MW00882868

To Sharon, the love of my life, who has stood by me for the past 33 years. Without her, I would not be the man I am today, and this book would not exist.

She has proofread each and every word with a keen and educated eye. Thank you, My Love, for enabling me to become just a little closer to the man my loving God would have me be.

All proceeds from this book will be donated to the Jeffersonville Token Club.

PREFACE

God brought this book into reality despite my lack of intention to write a daily meditation book or any other book.

Almost ten years ago, three or four dear friends and I decided it would be helpful if we made ourselves accountable to one another for having done our morning prayer and meditation by sending each other a text briefly referring to the morning's routine. One by one, the others dropped out, but by that time, a surprising number of people had asked to receive my daily text.

To my astonishment, I discovered that a substantial number of recipients were forwarding my text to 100 or more people. In time, I discovered that some people were translating the text into several different languages. This phenomenon is primarily the result of the efforts of my dear and cosmopolitan friend, John L.

The time required to send the text individually simply became overwhelming. My cherished and extremely talented friend, Cyndi M, and her associate, Mark S, discovered a way to send the daily text to many hundreds through a computer program.

As years went by, I began to refer to previous years and edit those more frequently than writing entirely new texts daily. Rather than laziness, it simply seemed that I had covered the major discoveries and experiences that have been most helpful to me.

Thus, my scribblings, by accident and the grace of God, morphed into a daily meditation book.

I believe this book differs from the multitude of meditation books on the market today in at least two regards. Number one, I have attempted to pass on, not so much what I have learned, as what I have done and found to work.

Number two, I do not believe the value of this book is limited to those involved in a recovery program, but rather, it is universally useful to anyone seeking to live a spiritual life.

In these pages, I fully acknowledge my inability to recognize perfection as well as my inability to attain it. Physical sobriety is the only thing I have done perfectly since my dry date of April 9, 1981. However, hopefully, my experience is a testament to the spiritual growth that flows from persistence, despite our inability to recognize or attain perfection. This truth is the basis of the title of the book, "Stumbling in the Right Direction."

You will note that each day begins with a "Keynote." These are simply spiritual principles or prayers chosen at random daily. Regardless of the particular "Keynote" chosen, I find that my behavior is more likely to be on a spiritual plane if I am concentrating on any spiritual principle or prayer.

The "Keynote" is not necessarily connected with the rest of the daily text, which is comprised of my thoughts on some part of my daily reading and prayer.

FOREWORD

by Bob B., St. Paul, Mn.

As many spiritual seekers before them, AA members have, since the earliest days, sought and found certain books which they read daily as part of their meditation practice. These, of course, include the Bible, the Sermon on the Mount, our own Big Book, and many other revered writings by Bill W. and other spiritual writings by both AA members and non-AA members.

In my 55 years of sobriety, I have benefited greatly from many of these daily readings. For the past roughly 10 years, Don has been distributing (via text) what has become the contents of "Stumbling in the Right Direction". I have been the beneficiary of Don's wisdom, and his writings have been a real support to me.

Don, who has been my friend for approximately 35 years, was an early prodigy, earning a law degree early and starting his own successful law firm only to lose it all to our disease. He lost his firm and law license, was divorced, and was estranged from his child for over three years. He ultimately became homeless on the streets and at the mercy of old friends.

About three years prior to his sobriety date of April 9, 1981, he was in a near-fatal car accident which resulted in 15 major surgeries. During the 21 months prior to Don's sobriety, he was institutionalized in psychiatric hospitals and treatment centers at least 18 times.

Upon finding the miracle of recovery, Don's law practice rebuilt and he has been happily married to Sharon for 33 years. He has a wonderful relationship with his children. The Bar Association, upon which his behavior brought such shame, has honored Don until he finds it an embarrassment.

In addition to spending 10 years on the state bar ethics committee, he has received the award for pro bono lawyer of the year and the award he treasures most of all, the award for professionalism and ethics.

Don is one of the smartest and most articulate men I have known. Of Don's many good qualities, the two which stand out the most are courtesy and persistence. He doesn't just teach these principles, he lives them. "Stumbling in the Right Direction" can be a great help, and I hope you find the writings of this forty-year sober practitioner of much insight and benefit as I have.

JANUARY

January 1

Happy New Year!

Our keynote is "Honesty".

The reading for this milestone day urges us to stay in the present moment and asks God to grant us the wisdom and strength needed just for the day.

When I sincerely seek to follow the Divine Spark's guidance, God never fails to fill my needs for the day. The problem is my desire for God to supply, on Sunday, the wisdom and strength necessary to handle Monday.

I have found asking God for protection from the future to be futile and disillusioning. As my friend, Leon, says, if I go into the future (or the past), I go alone. I am without God's protection from the monsters which I will surely find there.

My prayer for this New Year's Day is to live in the moment and not squander my life a minute at a time by wandering alone and afraid in the make-believe worlds of the future or the past.

God's Magic World exists only in the right now.

I love you all.

January 2

Good morning.

Our keynote is: "Humbly say to ourselves many times today, 'Thy will be done'..."

Today's Meditation and Prayer warn us not to make a big deal of the failures or triumphs of the past, whether they were five seconds or 50 years ago.

Making a big deal of past successes will lead to arrogance and resting on my laurels.

Past errors and transgressions will haunt and limit me until I do what I can to amend them.

That is why I must apply AA's 10th Step by PROMPTLY admitting my mistakes and acting to set them right. Then, I must forgive myself and move on. Refusing to forgive myself is not noble. It is a crippling character defect involving self-pity and "big dealism".

A few years ago, I stopped asking God to forgive me and to allow me to forgive myself. Instead, I began thanking God for having done so.

That little change in my daily prayer has magically helped me to more promptly and thoroughly leave the past where it belongs.

I love you all.

January 3

Good morning.

Today's keynote is: "Pray to seek to love, comfort, and understand..."

The Meditation and Prayer for the Day suggest we will be released from the bondage of our past by focusing on the right now and behaving as directed by the Divine Spark.

I am reminded of a conversation with a friend on the subject of "Learning to love oneself".

The first thing it brought to mind was how quickly I can devolve a mission to better love myself into just another form of self-obsession.

Upon reflection, I realized that only one course has ever added much to my affection for me. That is to behave lovingly toward others while ceasing to do unlovable things.

I tried to learn to love myself by studying, learning and praying. Standing alone, those endeavors resulted in little, if any, progress.

As always, doing the right things magically straightens out my thoughts, feelings, and beliefs.

Trying to mend my mind by more thinking has proved to be a fool's errand. Only kind and loving actions toward my fellows enable me to begin to love myself.

I love you all.

January 4

Good morning.

Our keynote is: "Help God's kids do what they need to have done..."

Today's Meditation and Prayer urge us to stay in this day and not try to shoulder the burden of the universe.

My ego wants to make a big deal out of my role in everything.

The truth is that I am almost never the star of the show and frequently don't even have a speaking part.

I need to remember that both my understanding of God's Will and my power are limited to my own next action.

It is also helpful for me to keep three questions in mind:

1. What is other people's business?
2. What is God's business?
3. What is my business?

When I honestly answer those questions, it is amazing how little is my business!

There is magic in being a bit player rather than the star.

I love you all.

January 5

Good morning.

Our keynote is "Kindness".

Today's reading discusses how God's presence in our lives brings us peace.

The essence of AA's Step 11 is seeking to remain conscious of God's presence, which has led me to call it the "peace step".

Starting and ending the day with prayer and meditation is extremely helpful. However, I find it even more important to use Step 11 throughout the other 95% of the day.

The Big Book's clear instructions for going through the day are as follows:

We pause when agitated or doubtful and ask for God's direction.

We constantly remind ourselves that we are no longer running the show.

We humbly say to ourselves many times each day, "Thy will be done".

Following those simple instructions is, magically, my key to a peaceful day. It also blesses me with the powerful and practical 11th Step promises of being more efficient and in much less danger of excitement, fear, anger, worry, self-pity, or foolish decisions.

I love you all.

January 6

Good morning.

Our keynote is "Kindness".

Discipline is the subject of today's Meditation and Prayer.

Lack of discipline has been my lifelong greatest shortcoming. Procrastination and, too frequently, obstinate refusal to do what needed to be done dominated my drinking life and are still prime sources of my fear.

In sobriety, I worked hard to become a disciplined person but made little progress because what I was actually trying to do was manage my life.

Great progress comes when I accept that I can neither manage my life nor discover some secret which will transform me into a disciplined person.

However, when I focus on heeding the Divine Spark with each stitch and think of others rather than myself, something magical happens; God disciplines me in the simple way outlined in AA's Big Book.

I may never become a disciplined person, but, one stitch at a time, I can behave like one. When doing so, I get all the benefits of being disciplined, and a casual observer might even get the impression that I have a modicum of self-discipline!

I love you all.

January 7

Good morning.

Our keynote is "Persistence".

Today's reading discusses temptation.

My experience in sobriety has changed my reaction to temptation. I thought wanting to do the wrong thing was a weakness or flaw.

In early sobriety, I believed if I could become spiritual enough, I would no longer feel tempted. As a result of realizing that my thoughts, feelings, and beliefs have no power unless I act on them, I no longer feel somehow flawed when presented with temptation.

We are all tempted.

In fact, I believe it to be a necessary element of growth. There is little spiritual value in not doing something I don't want to do. I believe the greatest spiritual growth comes from doing the next right thing when every fiber of my being wants to do the opposite.

I thank God that today I assess myself based on my behavior, rather than on what I want to do. I know the world judges me by that standard and suspect God does likewise.

Magical creatures in God's Magic World are tempted, and that's okay. Behaving better than I am tempted to behave is how I grow.

I love you all.

January 8

Good morning.

Our keynote is "Honesty".

Today's reading quotes St. Paul to the effect that our difficulties will become the basis of great things, including eventual peace and serenity.

That miracle happens for me, but only if I walk through difficulties by taking positive action consistent with faith. Otherwise, they are only difficulties, with no upside whatsoever.

My sobriety validates the principle. If I had not suffered through the nightmare of alcoholism, I would never have sought the path of spirituality.

In sobriety, having walked through embarrassing, painful, and persistent character defects is often the most helpful experience I have to share.

I never feel like exclaiming "Hooray!" when new difficulties approach. However, sometimes, I am able to behave like a person would behave if they welcomed those difficulties as spiritual exercise. To the extent I adopt that angle of approach, my difficulties are eased and bring about usefulness, which, in turn, brings peace and serenity.

I pray to see The Magic in my difficulties today.

I love you all.

January 9

Good morning.

Our keynote is: "Humbly say to ourselves many times today, 'Thy will be done...'"

Today's reading addresses faith.

Thinking and feeling that I am safe and secure in loving, Divine Hands brings me comfort and joy.

However, wishing, or even praying, without action, won't take me to the feeling of faith or keep me there.

In fact, I have come to believe that the warm, secure feeling is not faith; it is the reward for faith.

Experience has taught me that effective faith is action, and is sometimes temporarily difficult and frightening.

I have the greatest opportunities to be faithful when my mind and heart are most doubtful and fearful.

For me, real faith is heeding the Divine Spark with my next stitch when my mind tells me it won't work and my fear screams that I must look after myself.

When I stumble in that direction, God already has the situation in hand and the magical feeling we call faith returns.

I love you all.

January 10

Good morning.

Our keynote is: "Pray to seek to love, comfort, and understand..."

The Thought for the Day talks about the necessity for and the power of humility.

I never know whether I am humble because the instant I think I have humility, by definition, I do not.

Since I can never make a valid determination that I AM humble, how can I move toward that coveted and elusive goal?

We all know at least one person whose demeanor unmistakably whispers, "humility".

I choose such a role model and simply BEHAVE as I picture that person behaving in a situation similar to my own.

It is even easier to recognize an extreme lack of humility in others. I also choose one of those poor folks as a role model on what NOT to do or say.

I don't know whether behaving as a humble person will eventually mold me into one. But, I do know that persistently behaving humbly magically makes me more comfortable and effective. It also brings me closer to God and infuses my human interactions with love and gentleness.

I love you all.

January 11

Good morning.

Our keynote is: "Help God's kids do what they need to have done".

The Thought for the Day fits perfectly with today's keynote.

It stresses the importance of helping others and what a drastic change it is for many of us to focus on our fellows rather than ourselves.

AA's Big Book identifies selfishness and self-centeredness as the root of the alcoholic's problems.

Because the basis of my disorder is self-centeredness, I cannot effectively treat it by any form of obsession on self.

Perhaps the same is true of all people, alcoholic or not. My first sponsor taught me that selfishness is not peculiar to alcoholics; it is the disease of humankind.

Regardless of how I disguise and rationalize self-obsession, it remains as futile as trying to put out a fire with gasoline.

The core message of the Big Book is to stop thinking about myself so much and concentrate on helping others.

As Chuck C. said, it's not my job to take care of me. That is God's job. My job is trying to help God's kids do what they need to have done, for fun and for free, because I want to.

When I do my job, God magically always takes care of me.

I love you all.

January 12

Good morning.

Our keynote is "Kindness".

The Prayer for Today asks that we may be grateful for undeserved blessings and allow that gratitude to make us truly humble.

I believe gratitude necessarily brings humility. In fact, behaving in accord with any one spiritual principle or idea generally results in honoring all the others.

Regardless of which of our several keynotes is chosen for a day, if I persistently focus on it, I will behave much the same as if I had chosen any of the others. However, it is helpful to have a specific keynote each day to remind me that I am a spiritual and magical creature in God's Magic World.

Otherwise, I may irrevocably squander the day by taking the greatest possible gift for granted. I have sadly lost the joy of many days by throwing the precious gift of a day of human life back in God's face because I didn't like the way it was wrapped.

My daily reference to God's Magic is simply my way of expressing Sacred Awe. Being in awe of God and grateful for the gift of a day of human life magically transforms me and my perception of the world.

I love you all.

January 13

Good morning.

Our keynote is "Persistence".

Today's Meditation and Prayer encourage us to persevere while we are, "... being refined like gold in a crucible".

God takes me to better things when I persist in trying to do the next right thing during the darkest periods of my life. Those experiences with fear and despair ultimately become the foundation of the best parts of me. They are transformed into assets in helping others find the light in their dark days.

On the other hand, if I panic, obsess on myself and fail to take positive action, the darkness remains useless and continues to spiral me downward.

As I was once told by a successful professional poker player, at the end of the day, success or failure depends mainly on what we do with the worst hands we are dealt.

Taking the next stitch as the Divine Spark guides when my spirit is weakest is my path back to God's Magic.

I love you all.

January 14

Good morning.

Today's keynote is "Courtesy".

The Meditation for the Day stresses the importance of overcoming our selfishness. It tells us, "It is not the difficulties of life that I have to conquer, so much as my own selfishness".

I spent the first half of my life frantically running in the wrong direction, because I thought life's difficulties were the problem.

The key for me today is to not make a big deal of the constant stream of events in my life, whether I see them as good or bad. I often do more damage making big deals of events I see as positive than I do by blowing the negative out of proportion.

I am frequently wrong in my initial judgment of events anyway, so why get all worked up like a child on a roller coaster?

If I try to avoid big deals, seek to love, comfort and understand others and treat my selfishness as the root of my troubles, something magic happens.

As I concentrate on the next unselfish stitch, God takes care of the difficulties that my ego was screaming should demand all of my attention.

I love you all.

January 15

Good morning.

Our keynote is "Gratitude".

The Prayer for the Day implies that, by subjecting our wills to God's, we can, "...be free from all tenseness".

My first sponsor diagnosed me as suffering from a "disease of big deals", further describing it as a "Chicken Little Complex".

If an acorn hits you on the head, I think it's funny, but if it hits me, I think the sky is falling. My ego drastically inflates any event or circumstance that it can make about me.

The seemingly good big deals are at least as destructive as the ones I believe to be disastrous.

The truth is, anytime I make a big deal of anything that is not God or the 12 Steps, I am really making a big deal of myself. In doing so, I embrace my own will, robbing myself of peace, effectiveness, and often, rationality.

Big deals break my back and are the source of almost all my stress or tenseness.

I find The Magic by leaving the big deals to God and keeping only the really small ones for myself.

I love you all.

January 16

Good morning.

Today's keynote is "Humility".

The Meditation for the Day counsels perseverance in striving to do God's will in, "...the wilderness plains as well as the mountain tops of experience".

I tend to think, talk, and pray more about staying close to God in the wilderness, but the greater spiritual peril often lies on the mountain tops with my ego in overdrive.

It is easier for me to persistently feel the need for God when everything is in the ditch than when I think I am on top of the world.

I can also more clearly see the folly of having "big deals" in the difficult times. So, I desperately need to adhere to God's guidance in both the peaks and the valleys.

I pray today to persistently seek to take the next stitch as God directs, whether I view the situation as good or bad.

If I persistently stumble in that direction, I have a chance of consciously living in God's Magic today, regardless of the day's details and events.

I love you all.

January 17

Good morning.

Our keynote is "Honesty".

Today's Meditation and Prayer suggest using our attitude toward God and our fellows as protection against frets, impatience, worry, or "evil" thoughts.

I had always believed my "attitude" to be my mindset, or the way I thought and felt about some person, thing, or situation. Under that definition, my attitude was beyond my immediate control. I was enslaved to it.

In early sobriety, I was given a new definition of attitude, which is "angle of approach". Upon reading that definition, I experienced a life-changing epiphany. I realized that my angle of approach is the way I ACT toward someone or something. Under the "new" definition, my attitude instantly became totally within my control.

Since that moment, I have known that I can control my attitude and use it as a tool to maintain God consciousness and help me focus on others and what I can do for them.

When I use my "attitude" in that manner, frets, impatience, worry, and "evil" thoughts do, indeed, magically evaporate.

I love you all.

January 18

Good morning.

Our keynote is: "Help God's kids do what they need to have done,...".

Today's reading calls faith the basis for overcoming adverse conditions and accomplishing all good in our lives.

There are two distinct kinds of faith in my life today. One is the warm, secure feeling and belief that I am safely in God's hands. I used to believe such a state of mind and heart to be the only faith.

However, my experience has shown that I only get to that comfortable place through a second and more important form of faith, which is faithful action when my mind and heart are full of fear and doubt.

I cannot control the coming and going of the feeling of faith, but I have total control of my next action. Thus, I can BE faithful when I don't feel faithful.

There is little spiritual value in feeling all safe and secure. It never leaves a footprint on reality; it just makes me feel good.

But, magical results flow from persistently seeking to take the next faithful action when my mind and heart are not on board.

I love you all.

January 19

Good morning.

Our keynote is "Persistence".

According to today's Meditation, God anticipates our needs and is unimpressed with the eloquence or volume of our prayers.

In early sobriety, while behaving as a believer was leading me to belief and faith, I became concerned about the sincerity and quality of my prayers.

Often I did not want to pray, and my faith was so weak that I felt my prayers couldn't possibly be of any value.

Worse, I was frequently so scared and self-obsessed that I couldn't remember the last word I had prayed. Clearly, it seemed, the prayers were not going beyond the room.

In response to my concerns, I was told that God is already aware of my needs and doesn't need reminders or particular words in order to tend to them. I was also informed that I would not sway God with my eloquence.

It was explained that prayer is in no way a psychological or intellectual endeavor and will be ineffective if approached as such.

All the magic is in coming as a little child and humbling myself before my Creator to ask "please" and say "thank you".

I love you all.

January 20

Good morning.

Our keynote is "Kindness".

The Prayer for the Day asks that we may think love and health and, therefore, see and live within love and health.

In any community, there are people who believe and behave as if they live surrounded by loving, thoughtful, and helpful people who are trustworthy and reliable. In general, reality for those people is happily consistent with their belief and behavior.

Sadly, in the same community, some may believe they are constantly being slighted and double-crossed. Those benighted folks often see the motivations of others as malignant. For them, the community is a treacherous and miserable place to live.

The former group gives love, trust, honesty, and help. In return, they expect to and usually do receive the same. They live in God's Magic World and know that only their selfishness and fear block them from God's bounty.

When I behave like a person who seeks to give and expects to receive love, trust, honesty, and helpfulness, I magically live in a world filled with those very things.

I love you all.

January 21

Good morning.

Our keynote is "Persistence".

Today's Meditation and Prayer warn us to remain calm and not become upset during our crowded days.

My biggest hazard during busy days is my "big dealism". My ego wants to make a big deal out of anything that has to do with me. The truth is, anytime I make a big deal out of anything other than God, I am making a big deal out of myself.

Big deals impair my ability to focus and, worse, make it difficult for me to remain conscious of God. They swirl around in my head and prevent me from giving my entire interest, attention, and love to anything or anyone.

They make me forget that my job is to love, comfort, and understand others.

I can accomplish much more by taking one small, calm stitch at a time than by blowing my role in anything out of proportion.

There is no magic in my big deals. They bring stress, dramatically diminish efficiency, damage my relationships, and alienate me from God.

So, for today, I pray, "No big deals, please!".

I love you all.

January 22

Good morning.

Our keynote is "Courtesy".

Today's Meditation provides an effective lesson on the use of gratitude as a spiritual tool.

Gratitude is indispensable if I am to lead a better, more spiritual life. Yet, there are times when I simply do not feel thankful for the blessings God and the 12 steps shower on me. It is then that I must use gratitude as a tool by taking each stitch as a grateful person would until the feeling returns.

In fact, I believe when I act gratefully, I am grateful, regardless of my feelings. I also believe that if I feel grateful but am acting ungratefully, I have no effective gratitude.

Feeling grateful is often just the reward for behaving gratefully and the feeling alone won't keep me sober or have any impact on reality. It is my grateful action that keeps me sober and has a positive effect on the world around me.

The magic and reality are always in what I do, rather than what floats through my head.

I love you all.

January 23

Good morning.

Our keynote is: "Humbly say to ourselves many times today, 'Thy will be done',...".

Today's reading affirms the Big Book's message that lack of power is our dilemma, and God is the only source of the sorely needed power.

In order to access God's power, I must pray for it, but that is only the beginning.

I must accept that the only glimpse of God's will I ever get is for my own next action in the right now, and that my only power is over the next single stitch.

If I take that angle of approach and persist in trying to take the next stitch as the Divine Spark directs, God's power and grace flow into my life.

My God will do almost anything for me, but will do very little without my cooperation.

The magic is in the partnership of God's grace and power with my persistent faithful action.

I love you all.

January 24

Good morning.

Our keynote is "Humility".

Today's reading confirms that we cannot see the road ahead; our course will only be revealed one step at a time.

I have wasted far too many prayers imploring God to give me the knowledge and strength on Tuesday to handle Wednesday. It has never happened and never will.

My ego is chagrined to accept that I have spent so much of my life like an ant on a log floating down the river while believing it is steering the log.

That approach makes the ant (i.e., "me") ineffective, confused, self-absorbed, and frequently frantic.

I find the path to The Magic by accepting the limitations of my vision and power, leaving the patterns of my life to God, and following the guidance of the Divine Spark one stitch at a time.

The Divine Spark is not a road map charting my entire journey; it is more like a GPS unit directing me only one turn at a time.

I love you all.

January 25

Good morning.

Our keynote is "Honesty".

The Meditation for the Day declares, "...the foundation of serenity", to be complete surrender to God.

Applying yesterday's analogy, the ant has no chance for serenity unless it surrenders trying to steer the log.

We are also warned not to view this life as a constant struggle. One of my favorite gems of wisdom from Chuck C. is, "Whatever it is, if it's hard, I'm doing it wrong".

When I am able to completely surrender to God by accepting that I can control nothing but my own next stitch, I'm no longer a big deal.

It is my lack of humility in failing to accept my limitations which allows me to have big deals that are the archenemy of serenity.

But, when I come as a little child and behave as if I accept that I can't understand, much less control, the patterns of my life, something magical happens. Taking the next right stitch becomes relatively simple and easy.

Today I pray to realize that the stress always lies in my big deals, and serenity flows from making God the only big deal.

I love you all.

January 26

Good morning.

Our keynote is: "Humbly say to ourselves many times today, 'Thy will be done,...'".

Today's Meditation declares finding peace and acquiring serenity to be our great task.

However, it quickly clarifies that, while my own comfort will certainly be a byproduct of keeping my life calm and unruffled, it must never be the objective.

Instead, my soul must be calm so God's spirit can work through me to benefit others.

The origin of my alcoholism and all my spiritual maladies is self-centeredness.

Consequently, I can never effectively treat my flaws or shortcomings by any form of self-obsession.

Regardless of how I try to disguise self-obsession or what I name it, the result is still like trying to put out a fire with gasoline.

It is only through seeking to heal and comfort my fellows that I am healed and comforted by God's Magic.

Today, I pray to persistently think of God and to remain calm and unruffled so God's spirit can flow through me to others.

I love you all.

January 27

Good morning.

Our keynote is: "Pray to seek to love, comfort, and understand..."

Today's reading tells us that faith chases away fear, worry, and resentment.

Obviously, it is also true that fear, worry, and resentment preclude faith.

I have a mental picture of a single space inside me which I call my fear/faith container. The capacity of that container never changes. Therefore, precisely to the extent I have one, I cannot have the other.

The only way I have found to impact the balance between the positive and negative is through right action, including prayer. When my behavior is consistent with faith, my container fills with faith and its byproducts: peace, serenity, and joy.

However, when I fail or willfully refuse to stitch in accordance with the Divine Spark, the negativity of fear quickly pushes out faith and all of its benefits.

I pray today that the magic of right action will fill my container with faith.

I love you all.

January 28

Good morning.

Our keynote is: "Pray to seek to love, comfort, and understand..."

Today's reading advises us to follow and trust the "...way of the spirit" rather than the "...ways of the world."

In early sobriety, I was often told that allowing my comfort to depend on people, places, things, and situations would guarantee my discomfort.

Initially, I believed my mentors, but thought they meant that worldly matters often don't work out the way I want and/or envision.

Gradually, I came to realize that the admonition is far more profound and serious.

I now realize that making the spiritual mistake of letting my comfort depend on human behavior and worldly events assures my eventual emptiness and disillusionment, regardless of how those things unfold.

That is the inevitable result of trying to fill the God-shaped hole in my soul with something other than God.

Today, I pray to leave my comfort and wellbeing in God's steady hands rather than in the weak and fickle hands of the world. By doing so, I can hope to live this day in The Magic of faith.

I love you all.

January 29

Good morning.

Today's keynote is: "Help God's kids do what they need to have done..."

The Meditation and Prayer for the Day describe the relationship between God and the individual, as God being the architect and we the builders.

This is the same "simple idea" that, in writing about AA's third step, Bill W. repeats four times and calls "...the keystone of the arch through which we walk to freedom."

The Great Architect's plan for my life is only revealed one single brick or nail at a time through the Divine Spark.

If I ignore or reject God's plan, the only possible result is chaos and futility. But if I persistently try to heed the Divine Spark, I am often able to look back and think, "Wow! Who would have thought that God would plan anything so beautiful for me!"

The Magic always flows from adding my persistent, faithful action, one stitch at a time, to God's Grace, Power, and secret plans.

I love you all.

January 30

Good morning.

Our keynote is "Kindness."

The Meditation for the Day promises that God will never give us a load greater than we can bear and that true success lies in serenity and peace.

Serenity and peace rarely crossed my mind in the old days. I would have assumed they came primarily assisted by alcohol. I would have also thought they might come after I had navigated my big deals successfully and wrested what I wanted from the grip of an unwilling universe.

I had no idea that seeking to remain calm, peaceful, and serene would produce success in every area of my life.

I thought assuming the burden of many tomorrows, as well as responsibility for the results of my efforts, was necessary for material success.

That angle of approach resulted in loads I could not bear.

I find The Magic, peace, serenity, and success by staying in the moment, having only little deals, and giving my entire interest, attention, and love to whomever or whatever is directly in front of me.

I love you all.

January 31

Good morning.

Our keynote is "Persistence".

Today's Meditation and Prayer are a road map for navigating the lowest, most painful times in life. We are urged to continue to say, "Thy will be done," and persist in trying to take the next right stitch when we are full of fear and doubt.

A successful professional poker player once told me that whether he ultimately won or lost depended on how he played the worst hands he was dealt.

Experience has validated that principle in every area of my life.

It's relatively easy to do the next right thing when the future looks bright and I'm full of faith, confidence, and trust in God.

However, while there is great freedom and joy in feeling like doing the right thing, there is little spiritual growth.

It is when my faith is weakest, fear is upon me, and the situation looks hopeless that DOING the faith which I do not feel will lead me back to God's Magic.

It is what I do while in the "midnights of my soul" that will, in the end, determine whether I succeed or fail.

I love you all.

FEBRUARY

February 1

Good morning.

Our keynote is "Courtesy."

The Thought for the Day addresses the short-sightedness of an alcoholic picking up the first drink. At that moment, we ignore the certain avalanche of negativity which must result from seeking a fleeting bit of euphoria. It is, quite simply, an insane decision.

In my experience, this particular brand of insanity is not limited to alcoholics and drinking. Even though I haven't drunk for many years, I still tend to do things which cost far more than they are worth.

Procrastination, for example, ensures pain out of all proportion to the difficulty of the neglected task. Likewise, spending too much money on unneeded things brings remorse, guilt, and financial consequences wildly outweighing the pleasure of the acquisition.

I am so lacking in self-discipline that I must let God discipline me through the 12 steps.

By God's grace, if I live the steps and persistently obey the Divine Spark, one stitch at a time, God will provide the missing discipline. I will once again consciously walk in The Magic.

I love you all.

February 2

Good morning.

Our keynote is "Gratitude."

Today's reading is about love and behaving lovingly.

Feeling love is uplifting, joyful, and makes it easier to behave lovingly. However, in and of itself, my loving feeling doesn't do much for other people or to enhance my spiritual life.

The promise of today's reading is that by behaving lovingly, I will ultimately live in love.

It is especially important that I act lovingly toward those for whom I don't feel love. Frequently, doing loving things for the unlovable will magically bring the freedom and joy of feeling love for them.

Also, real love from my fellows often comes back to me as a byproduct of my efforts to love them.

Love is not just part of spirituality; it may very well be the whole of spirituality.

It is impossible for me to be spiritual while behaving in an unloving manner.

If God is Love, then Love itself is God.

I love you all.

February 3

Good morning.

Our keynote is "Humility."

The Meditation for the Day confirms my experience that God's Power, coupled with my faithful action, can accomplish anything in human relations.

However, God doesn't bless interaction with my fellows unless I do the footwork, such as:

1. Praying, before and during each human interaction, to seek to love, comfort, and understand, and NOT to seek love, comfort, and understanding for myself.
2. Being persistently courteous (discourtesy precludes God's presence).
3. Seeking to give my entire interest, attention, and love to whomever is in front of me.
4. Remembering that unsolicited advice is always criticism; no exceptions.
5. Asking what I can bring to each situation, rather than what I can gain from it.

If I persistently approach human encounters in that manner, they magically are easier, more harmonious, and mutually rewarding.

I love you all.

February 4

Good morning.

Our keynote is "Honesty with compassion."

Today's reading examines the alcoholic's use of drinking as a crutch.

Seeking satisfaction and peace through alcohol is an extreme example of letting one's comfort depend on something or someone other than God. Such an attempt doesn't work in any form.

The Big Book says that deep down in every man, woman, and child is the idea of God. Expanding on that, I have heard it said that in each one of us, there is a God-shaped hole, which can be filled by nothing but God.

All my frantic efforts to ignore that need and seek refuge and satisfaction elsewhere resulted only in chaos and destruction.

Childlike dependence on God is the very foundation of recovery in AA and the spiritual life.

Once I heard a newly sober AA member recount that his wife had told him that AA is just a crutch. The fellow told her, "Well, I reckon a crutch ain't a bad thing if you're crippled."

God has all The Magic.

Seeking it elsewhere is a fool's errand.

I love you all.

February 5

Good morning.

Our keynote is "Humbly say to ourselves many times each day, 'Thy will be done',...".

Today's Meditation and Prayer are about persisting along the path of spirituality and the 12 steps.

I view "persisting" as quite different from "continuing," which connotes never straying from the path.

"Persisting," on the other hand, presumes repeatedly failing and starting over.

Today's reading affirms the inevitability of encountering periods during which I feel cut off from God, AA, and spirituality. In those gray times, I can't wave a wand and change my thoughts, feelings, or beliefs.

What I can do is persist in actions consistent with faith.

However faint the Divine Spark may seem, I can do my best to take the next stitch as directed. If I persist in doing so while trudging through those spiritual twilights, my actions will eventually restore my mind, heart, and soul. I will once again become aware of and, therefore, consciously part of God's Magic.

I love you all.

February 6

Good morning.

Our keynote is: "Pray to seek to love, comfort, and understand..."

According to the Meditation for the Day, God finds, amid the crowd, a few people who persistently seek to live in the presence of The Divine.

It reminds me of a conversation my original sponsor had with Bill Wilson. Bill said about 95% of the people who succeed in AA do enough to stay sober and have good lives. Those folks are, indeed, good AA members, Bill said.

But he continued, about 5% want it all. They want all possible peace, spirituality, and harmony with God and their fellows. I suspect this divide applies to all who profess spirituality, not just AA members.

From the day I heard that story, I have longed to be part of the 5%. I am convinced that whether I am part of the 5% or the 95% at any given time depends primarily on my behavior that day.

To have a chance of experiencing the magic of being in the 5%, I must remain conscious of God, treat my fellows well, and stitch as the Divine Spark directs.

I love you all.

February 7

Good morning.

Our keynote is: "Help God's kids do what they need to have done..."

The Thought for the Day urges us to think less about the pleasure of our contemplated actions and more about their consequences.

My perception disorder makes the warning especially ominous.

At an AA conference, I heard a song entitled, "Trouble Always Starts Out Looking Like Fun."

My insane ideas never introduce themselves as crazy notions that might destroy my life. They present as fun and/or common sense. Because of the disorder of my perception, I am apt to believe them!

My first sponsor held that we always get the divinely perfect consequences of our actions. Sometimes my actions open the door to The Magic and other times they plunge me into chaos. Therefore, it is critical that I persistently seek and follow the guidance of the Divine Spark.

The Spark always directs action that leads to The Magic and never to chaos! Unlike my mind, it never lies to me.

I love you all.

February 8

Good morning.

Our keynote is "Kindness".

Today's Meditation and Prayer counsel patience and waiting for God's guidance rather than acting rashly.

An early AA mentor called the idea, "Do something, even if it's wrong.", the most insane premise on which he conducted his life before sobriety.

In my own life, I have gotten into, and caused, far more trouble by acting rashly or speaking too soon than by remaining quiet and still when uncertain of my next word or action.

I must depend on God to find the balance between rash or premature activity on one hand and paralysis from indecision on the other.

If I could find that balance on my own, I could manage my life.

History makes it clear that I can do neither.

The magic is in waiting for the Divine Spark's guidance, but acting promptly, in spite of fear and my propensity to procrastinate, when the next stitch becomes clear.

I love you all.

February 9

Good morning.

Our keynote is "Persistence".

The Prayer for the Day asks that no lack of trust or fearfulness will make us disloyal to God.

The prayer assumes that we WILL, at times, not feel trust in God and will be afraid to do what we know in our hearts is right.

Happily, it also strongly implies that such feelings do not constitute disloyalty to God.

The fluctuations of the old crazy picture show in my head don't make me either disloyal or loyal. Whether I am loyal to God (or my fellows) will be determined solely by what I do and fail to do.

Today, I pray that my actions will be loyal to God, even if fear has caused my mind to doubt and my feelings of faith and trust to falter.

As ever, The Magic is in the action; not in my shifting and fickle thoughts, feelings, and beliefs.

I am grateful that my loyalty is measured by my behavior, which I can control, and not by the crazy picture show in my head, which I cannot immediately control.

I love you all.

February 10

Good morning.

Our keynote is "Courtesy".

The Meditation for the Day compares us to trees that must be pruned of dead branches in order to bear good fruit. It goes on to assure that we are in the hands of a Master Gardener who makes no mistakes in pruning.

I am reminded of my inability to change myself. I can, and must, change my behavior, but it is God who must change who and what I am.

I don't even know which branches need to be pruned, much less when or how.

As always, I must come as a little child, stumbling along while holding the Divine Hand and trying to take the next stitch as directed.

If I persistently and faithfully stitch, God's grace and power will gradually grow me into something closer to the Divine Vision of who and what I should be.

The Magic is never in my self-determined objectives. It is always in God's perfect objectives, which I am never able to see or comprehend.

I love you all.

February 11

Good morning.

Our keynote is "Gratitude".

Today's reading stresses the importance of waiting patiently for God's guidance. It warns that too much unguided and frantic activity will mar our work and spiritually hobble us.

I need to be mindful of the difference between activity and action.

Activity is speaking and acting (often rashly and frantically) without sufficient aforethought or consciousness of God. In so acting, I am usually motivated by fear or some other manifestation of self. My mind is clouded and my soul diminished. I am robbed of effectiveness, peace, and the ability to properly consider the impact of my behavior on others.

Action, on the other hand, is patiently seeking to do the right thing, as guided by the Divine Spark. With that angle of approach, I am moved toward effectiveness, peace, harmony with my fellows, and awareness of God's Magic.

I pray today to take quiet, prayerful action and avoid frantic and/or aimless activity that corrodes my soul.

I love you all.

February 12

Good morning.

Our keynote is "Humility".

The Meditation and Prayer for the Day are completely devoted to the importance of persistent awareness of God.

In the course of many annual trips through the 24 Hour Book, I have noticed that the same themes are repeated over and over. The two most frequently emphasized are remaining conscious of God and helping others.

The reason they are so often the heart of the daily reading is no mystery. If I maintain God consciousness and stay focused on what I can do for others, it's not necessary to complicate things beyond that.

Just to the extent that I do those two things, I will be useful, efficient, have peace, and not be dominated by fear.

That straightforward but often difficult to maintain approach IS the spiritual life.

Magically, the key to it all really is that simple.

I love you all.

February 13

Good morning.

Our keynote is "Honesty".

Today's Meditation and Prayer never mention the word "persistence", but it is the heart of their message.

We are warned against giving up when things appear hopeless. This is critical in my life. I believe the most lethal weapon in the arsenal of my alcoholic ego is convincing me that there is no longer any use in trying. It tells me I am so far off track there is no longer a next right stitch.

That is a lie. There is always a next right thing to do, even in the middle of robbing a bank! I can't get far enough from God's will that the Divine Spark is inaccessible.

In both the spiritual and material realms, my most ultimately successful endeavors have frequently, at some point, felt completely hopeless.

Human weakness and failure are part of God's will, and persistently returning to the right action, in spite of them, leads to The Magic!

I love you all.

February 14

Our keynote is: "Humbly say to ourselves many times today, 'Thy will be done'...".

The Meditation for the Day suggests that our spiritual growth and healing come more from persistent awareness of God than from prayer itself.

In early sobriety, I was told that my willingness to humble myself before God is far more important than any eloquent prayers I may craft.

My morning and evening routines have long included praying on my knees and then quietly seeking God's guidance. I suspect God doesn't care how my body is positioned when I pray. I get on my knees morning and night, not so much for God as for myself.

The physical act of humbling myself before my Creator makes me more receptive to Divine Guidance, fosters God consciousness throughout the day, and gives me clarity in reviewing my behavior at day's end.

Praying on my knees affirms my surrender to God, makes me more aware of God's Magic, and helps me maintain Sacred Awe.

I love you all.

February 15

Good morning.

Our keynote is "Pray to seek to love, comfort and understand...".

The Meditation and Prayer for the Day urge us to be instruments of the Divine Power and the forces for good.

Interestingly, they tell us that God needs "supernatural" people.

That statement assumes selfishness to be human nature. My first sponsor called self-centeredness, which is at the core of my alcoholism, the disease of all humankind.

At least at first, obeying the Divine Spark while my brain and ego scream that it is against our self-interest is not natural.

The only way I have found to be lifted above my nature and ego is by trying to take correct stitches in spite of it feeling unnatural. Magically, the more supernatural stitches I take, the more natural they begin to feel.

If my selfish nature is to be overcome, I must persistently behave better than my instincts, which allows God to slowly transform my nature.

I love you all.

February 16

Good morning.

Our keynote is: "Help God's kids do what they need to have done...".

Today's Meditation urges us to remain calm regardless of what is going on around us.

Morning prayer and quiet communion with God are necessary preparations for a calm day. They are, however, only a start.

If I am to remain calm, even when my world turns chaotic and threatening, I need to:

1. Live the other 95% of step 11 by seeking to remain God conscious throughout the day.

2. Have no big deals.

3. Not procrastinate.

4. Be rigorously, but compassionately, honest.

5. Promptly make amends and 10th Step admissions of wrongdoing.

6. Pray to love, comfort and understand others, instead of seeking those things for myself.

Multiple times every day I fail to perfectly adhere to those goals. However, persistently returning to them is magically sufficient to allow God to keep me calm in the midst of life's storms.

I love you all.

February 17

Good morning.

Our keynote is: "Persistence".

Today's Meditation emphasizes that drawing nearer to God in quiet communion is the purpose and goal of all worship.

I agree, but experience has convinced me that prayer and meditation are interdependent with my actions and, specifically, with my treatment of God's children.

The more my behavior is in sync with God's will, the easier it is for me to draw close to God in prayer and meditation. Gratefully, it's not necessary for me to have "clean hands" in order to connect with God, but I must be striving to have them in order to effectively do so.

Conversely, seeking God through prayer and meditation clears my channel with the Divine Spark, which makes it easier for me to act in harmony with God's will and treat my fellows well.

It is another example of the magic which flows from the joining of God's power and grace with our faithful actions.

I love you all.

February 18

Good morning.

Our keynote is "Courtesy."

Today's meditation suggests trusting God as a little child trusts their mother in handing her a tangled ball of yarn.

I remember being that child. I had no doubt that Mama would straighten out my mess, and there was no reluctance to turn it over to her. She was my loving mother and, in my child's mind, could and would do anything for me.

However, she couldn't help until I accepted the mess as being beyond my abilities and took the action of bringing it to her. It is the same with turning my grown-up messes over to God. I don't turn things over to God by merely saying, "God, it is yours." They are turned over by my persistent, faithful action or not at all.

The only way to turn a toothache over to God is by going to a dentist.

When I fail or refuse to behave as the Divine Spark directs, I create, keep, or take back my tangled messes.

So much of God's Magic flows from coming as a little child!

I love you all.

February 19

Good morning.

Our keynote is "Gratitude."

The Meditation for the Day advises us to "endure to the very end."

The reference to endurance (i.e., persistence) brings back yesterday's mental picture of my four-year-old self giving my hopelessly tangled yarn to my mother.

I see myself drying my eyes and being greatly relieved at first. But then, I imagine Mama not immediately dropping everything to untangle the yarn to my expectations.

Even though I made the mess (and threw a hissy fit over my inability to fix it), I begin to think I can do the job better than my mother.

She lays aside the yarn to tend to something else.

Of course, I pick it up and proceed to undo all her progress and make the mess worse than ever.

The magic doesn't come by merely placing my problems in God's hands. I must leave them there, especially when I believe God isn't doing the job correctly or quickly enough!!

I love you all.

February 20

Good morning.

Our keynote is "Humility."

The Meditation for the Day assures us that we can depend on God to supply all the power we need to face any situation.

But, it continues, the Power can only be accessed if we are seeking to do God's will, one stitch at a time.

I also frequently need reminding that God only supplies my needs in the present.

I have wasted much time and effort seeking the strength to endure the future.

Mark Twain said, "My life has been filled with many tragedies, almost none of which ever happened."

Similarly, my friend, Leon, warns that if I go into the future, God says, "Have a good time. I will be here when you get back."

Today, I pray to accept that I am constructed to carry only the burdens of the present.

I never find The Power or The Magic in the future or the past; only in the right now.

I love you all.

February 21

Good morning.

Our keynote is "Honesty".

Today's Meditation warns that soul disturbance can be a greater danger than fire or earthquake.

I don't believe that to be an overstatement.

During "soul storms", I can be just as dangerous to others and myself as I was drunk.

It is no coincidence that we use the word "mad" to describe both being angry and being insane.

In the clutches of anger, big deals, and/or madness, I am robbed of reason, compassion, and awareness of the Divine Spark.

I pray today that I may avoid big deals and, at the first gust of a soul storm, ask myself, "How important is it really, compared to my emotional sobriety?"

The Magic can only be seen with a peaceful heart and through calm eyes.

I love you all.

February 22

Good morning.

Our keynote is: "Humbly say to ourselves many times today, 'Thy will be done'...".

The Meditation for the Day warns against failing God because of our doubts and fears.

Just as it is with faith and gratitude, I have no immediate control over feeling trust in God.

However, I don't believe I fail God just because my thoughts, feelings, and beliefs are clouded by doubt. I fail God, others, and myself only when I allow waning mental faith to prevent me from behaving as the Divine Spark directs.

My God gives me control over only one thing in this universe, which is my own next action.

God does not give me immediate control over my mind, and, based on my experience, does not judge me on something I cannot control.

If I persist in taking my next action as one who trusts God would do, I am trusting in God, regardless of what is going on in my mind.

The person I am, to the world and God, is defined solely by my actions, not the crazy picture show in my head.

By behaving trustingly, I enjoy all the magic of trust and am eventually returned to the comfort of feeling that trust.

I love you all.

February 23

Good morning.

Our keynote is: "Pray to seek to love, comfort, and understand...".

Today's Meditation tells us the busy life is a joyful life and is to be loved.

Some of my extremely busy times have been useful, productive, joyful, and peaceful. Others have felt like a chaotic living hell in which I was under attack from every direction.

Looking back, one factor always determines which of those two busy worlds I inhabit. That factor, of course, is whether I am conscious of God being in charge or am floundering in the delusion of control.

When my ego convinces me that I am in charge, I am like an ant floating down a river on a log believing it is steering the log. Such a hapless ant will know neither peace nor success.

Conscious contact with God clears my mind of the delusion that I must or can "steer the log". It IS The Magic!

I love you all.

February 24

Good morning.

Our keynote is: "Help God's kids do what they need to have done".

The Meditation and Prayer for the Day urge us to treat each person who crosses our path as if they were sent by God.

It reminds me that a few years ago I added to my morning prayer a request for help in trying to make the day a little brighter for everyone I encounter. This includes the people closest to me as well as strangers in fleeting encounters.

Sometimes a mere smile or letting someone know they are seen as a person can brighten the day of a fellow human being.

My part in treating my fellows as if they are sent by God begins with courtesy.

In my experience, courtesy is the single most underestimated spiritual trait. I believe it is impossible for me to be discourteous and spiritual at the same time.

Courtesy carries the message of God's love and makes people comfortable in approaching me for help.

It is magic in human relations.

I love you all.

February 25

Good morning.

Our keynote is "Courtesy".

Today's Meditation and Prayer declare faith, fellowship, and service to be the cure for most of the world's ills.

I was prompted to wonder whether I am part of the world's ills or part of the cure.

My conclusion is that, in the course of most days, I am both.

Whether I carry healing or illness depends upon what I am doing, or not doing, at any given moment.

When I allow my self-centered nature to control my actions, there is apt to be a little more darkness in the universe. It is certain that, with each selfish and inconsiderate stitch, the light within me dims.

However, when I am responsive to the Divine Spark and seek to love, comfort, and understand my fellows, there is one more pinpoint of light in the world, and the Sunlight of the Spirit brightens my own soul.

Whether I smile or glower at the next person I encounter may actually impact the balance between the world's ills and its cure.

It will surely impact whether I walk in darkness or in The Magic.

I love you all.

February 26

Good morning.

Our keynote is "Humility".

Today's reading urges us to REALIZE that God has, and wants to give us, everything we need, and that it is only our selfishness which blocks God's bounty.

To "realize" is very different than to "know". It literally means to make something real.

I give reality to being a beloved child of God by behaving like one.

Each day, I have a choice of angles of approach. I can live in a selfish and hostile universe, trying to wrest my needs from its unwilling grip, or I can live as a magical creature in God's magic and bountiful world.

I can form an intention to live in the better world, but if it is to become real, I must then persistently behave as one living in that unselfish and loving world of plenty. Only then does my intention achieve reality by graduating to a decision.

I love you all.

February 27

Good morning.

Our keynote is "Honesty".

Today's reading assures us that conscious contact with God will relieve all our resentment, worry, and fear. Calmed and guided by contact with The Divine, we will be able to go about our real purpose of being helpful to others.

In my experience, the closest thing I have found to the panacea is awareness of my Creator. However, if I am to keep my mind on God and off myself, I must take action. I need to say to myself many times each day, "Thy will be done".

I benefit from holding the door to a room or car just an extra beat for God to enter.

Other simple reminders, like a rubber band around my wrist or a wadded piece of paper in my pocket, have often pulled me back from the abyss of self-centered chaos to God's peace and usefulness.

Dropping to my knees for a few seconds to start a day over has calmed many a soul storm.

Persistently thinking of God is my key to The Magic.

I love you all.

February 28

Good morning.

Our keynote is: "Humbly say to ourselves many times each day 'Thy Will be done'..."

Today's reading tells us that spiritual preparation makes us more efficient and effective in any endeavor.

Before sobriety, spirituality seemed impractical and of little, if any, utility in addressing my daily responsibilities.

As with so many things, I had it completely backward.

Experience has convinced me that spiritual preparation is always the most practical thing I can do.

It often makes the difference between frantic, inefficient activity and precise, effective action.

The magic is in putting the spiritual first. When I choose that angle of approach, my material world usually falls into place.

However, if I allow the material to be my primary focus and the spiritual merely a sideshow, I rarely have much success in either realm.

Putting spirituality first has proved to magically serve my best interest in business and every walk of life.

I love you all.

MARCH

March 1

Good morning.

Our keynote is: "Help God's kids do what they need to have done".

Today's reading tells us that constant effort is necessary to maintain the all-important conscious contact with God. It emphasizes the importance of PERSISTENCE, which is at the heart of my sobriety and spiritual journey.

I can't get close to always stitching in accord with the Divine Spark or remaining aware of God every waking moment. Being human, perfection is not in my toolbox. Many times each day, I lose my God consciousness and veer off on a tangent of self-will.

What I CAN do is persistently return to seeking conscious contact with God and stitching as the Divine Spark directs. Falling away from the spiritual path, but persistently recognizing my lapse and taking another couple of correct stitches, is the only spiritual progress of which I am capable.

The Magic is that my God doesn't require perfection but seems quite pleased with persistence!

I love you all.

March 2

Good morning.

Our keynote is "Persistence".

The Meditation for the Day continues to stress the power of seeking connection with God. In discussing Step 11, the AA Big Book directs us to pause when agitated or doubtful, ask for guidance, humbly say to ourselves many times each day, "Thy will be done", and constantly remind ourselves that we are no longer running the show. We are assured that following those clear and simple directions throughout each day will trigger the beautifully practical 11th Step Promises. They include being in much less danger of excitement, fear, anger, worry, self-pity, or foolish decisions and becoming much more efficient.

My brain and ego tell me that such a simple formula could not possibly bring about those massive positive changes. However, my experience confirms that "It works. It really does!"

Persistently following those directions gives me a much better chance of consciously living today as a magical creature in God's Magic World.

I love you all.

March 3

Good morning.

Our keynote is "Courtesy".

Today's reading emphasizes that thinking often of spiritual things will bring unconscious growth all by itself. It goes on to affirm my own experience by warning that we will often have a sense of failure in our efforts to focus on God and the spiritual.

I sometimes feel I am failing so miserably in maintaining God consciousness that I will never make any real progress. If I allow that feeling of hopelessness to dictate my behavior, I am lost. I will cease to persist in trying to heed the Divine Spark and will be on a fast track to the abyss.

However, if I persist in coming back to God's guidance, despite my feelings of hopeless failure, God's Magic intervenes. My faithful behavior, coupled with God's grace and power, replaces hopelessness with faith.

God, not I, is the judge of my spiritual progress. I am far better served by persisting in God-guided action than by constantly taking my spiritual temperature.

I love you all.

March 4

Good morning.

Our keynote is "Gratitude".

The Meditation for the Day opens with this powerful declaration: "The elimination of selfishness is the key to happiness and can only be accomplished with God's help".

Before sobriety, my purpose in life was to make myself happy. But the harder I tried, the more elusive real happiness became. The first thing wrong with me is selfishness and self-centeredness. My alcoholism and most of my difficulties spring from that core defect.

I can never effectively address this overarching flaw by any form of self-obsession. The magic happens when I stop seeking my own happiness, give up on fixing myself, and start acting out of concern for others. Only then do I find harmony with God and my fellows. As a byproduct of unselfish action and taking one faithful stitch after another, happiness finds me.

I love you all.

March 5

Good morning.

Our keynote is "Humility."

The Thought for the Day suggests that alcoholics sometimes make the AA program too hard. In my case, it is only hard when I fail to "come as a little child" and, instead, try to comprehend it all and fix myself. My ego and intellect tell me that all of life is difficult and complicated; that it requires all of my wit, guile, and toughness. If I embrace that attitude, my life is dominated by an endless stream of stressful and difficult "big deals."

In reality, I get better results from Chuck C's angle of approach, "Regardless of what it is, if it is hard, I am doing it wrong."

Realizing Chuck's wisdom in that declaration begins with acceptance and humility. Accepting that my knowledge of God's will and my human power are both limited to only my own next action simplifies my life and makes the next right thing clearer and easier to do.

As I stumble forward with that acceptance, everything becomes progressively easier. If I persist, God's grace and power magically produce divinely perfect results with little difficulty and no "big deals" on my part.

I love you all.

March 6

Good morning.

Our keynote is "Honesty."

The Meditation and Prayer for the day emphasize that we must work for, with, and through God. I must work with God because most of the blessings in my life flow from the partnership of God's power and grace with my faithful action. Since my own power is so extremely limited, I must work through God in order to benefit from the Divine Power. However, it has served me well to primarily concentrate on working FOR God.

If I think too much in terms of working WITH God, I may decide I'm an equal partner and that God needs my input. If I focus on working THROUGH God, I may think I am the CEO of my life and reduce God to a tool for pursuing my own will.

It benefits me to stand before a mirror in the morning and salute while saying aloud, "Good morning, God! Private Don M. reporting for duty!"

I find The Magic by seeking to be God's simple, unquestioning servant.

I love you all.

March 7

Good morning.

Our keynote is: "Humbly say to ourselves many times today, 'Thy will be done'..."

The Prayer for the Day asks that I may do God's will in all my affairs and try to help others find God's will for themselves.

If I am to do God's will, I must be attentive to the Divine Spark and try to take the next stitch (i.e., action) as It directs. I have no other conduit to God's will. The only guidance God gives me is for my own very next action, and my power in this world is limited to that single next stitch.

I must try to carry the message by helping others find God's will for themselves. I can seek to demonstrate and tell how I connect with and receive guidance from the Divine Spark, but I must never play God by presuming to know God's will for another person.

The Magic happens when I tend to my own stitching and stand ready to help my fellows find the Divine Spark within themselves.

I love you all.

March 8

Good morning.

Our keynote is: "Pray to seek to love, comfort, and understand..."

Today's Meditation and Prayer stress the importance of spiritual fellowship.

AA's worldwide success is largely based on alcoholics banding together in support of their mutual quest for recovery.

However, the value of spiritual fellowship is by no means limited to alcoholics. It is written that where two or three spiritually minded people come together, God will also be there.

When besieged by potentially catastrophic insane ideas, my fellows have often been my salvation.

My crazy ideas never tell me, "I am an insane idea and I am here to kill you." Instead, they whisper that they are common sense and are here to help. Due to the disorder of my perception, I am in constant danger of believing my insane ideas to be common sense.

Seeking input from my fellows protects me from my mind and ego.

Magically, my insane ideas never sound like common sense to you, and yours never sound like common sense to me.

I love you all.

March 9

Good morning.

Our keynote is: "Help God's kids do what they need to have done..."

Today's Meditation and Prayer declare the most valuable life to be one of honesty, purity, unselfishness, and love.

In early sobriety, I would often hear someone say, "My worst day sober is better than my best day drinking". It would embarrass and frighten me because I surely couldn't agree.

Gradually, I came to realize that my obsession with how I feel was causing me to hear them say they felt better on their worst day sober than they FELT on their best day drinking.

Then I began to realize that the bedrock of my alcoholism (and most of my troubles) is this... without Divine Intervention, I will always wind up letting how I feel be the most important thing in the world.

Now I seek to value my days based on what I do rather than how I feel. The world and, I believe, God have always judged me by that standard alone.

Magically, I can now agree that my worst day sober is a better, more valuable day than my best day drinking.

I love you all.

March 10

Good morning.

Our keynote is "Persistence".

The Prayer for the Day asks that my spirit may be in tune with the Spirit of the universe.

Each morning when I awaken, the universe is playing a unique symphony divinely composed for that day.

My long experience with fruitlessly trying to manipulate God's will has taught me that the universe does not take requests.

I can never change a note of the Great Composer's program for the day.

Each morning I must make a simple choice.

I can either dance to the music of the spheres or sulk in the corner between temper tantrums.

The only course that brings me in tune with the universe is to behave gratefully while heeding the Divine Spark, one stitch at a time.

I am more useful and my days are much more peaceful when I embrace the music God has ordained, rather than skittering around to my ego's cacophony.

God's Magic finds me when I come as a little child and accept the world exactly as it is today.

I love you all.

March 11

Good morning.

Our keynote is "Courtesy".

Today's reading evokes the beauty of character found in some of our fellows.

Many times I am uncertain how to be a good friend, sponsor, AA member, father, husband, lawyer, or person.

Praying for guidance is a necessary starting point, but the Divine Spark frequently brings to my mind someone who is clearly blessed and adept at the particular role in which I find myself.

Often I am shown the next stitch by bringing up a mental picture of one who appears to be as I wish to be.

If I emulate those precious examples, I have a chance of growing to resemble them.

Today I pray to behave like my role models whose behavior whispers humility and awareness of being a loving, and loved, magical creature in God's Magic World.

Thank God for those who guide me by example.

I love you all.

March 12

Good morning.

Our keynote is "Gratitude".

Today's Meditation and Prayer declare simplicity to be the basis of a good life.

While my experience validates that idea, simplicity seems to offend my brain and ego. They constantly urge me to complicate and acquire.

Much progress has come from considering simplicity in every choice with which I am presented. At each of the many little crossroads in the course of a day, I need to ask myself which choice is simpler and let that be a factor in my decision. If I persist along that path, God will simplify my life.

I have found no other effective route to simplification other than persistently choosing the less complicated path.

Very importantly, if I know my answer is "No", I need to quickly say so. Otherwise, my ego will cause me to prevaricate and procrastinate until the situation grows into a monster.

Finally, I need to remember the proverb, "There is no greater tragedy than lavish desires".

I find The Magic in simplicity; never in complication and extravagance.

I love you all.

March 13

Good morning.

Our keynote is "Humility".

Today's reading promises that bringing our spirits into harmony with God's Spirit will result in limitless possibilities in the realm of human relationships.

The Prayer of St. Francis is my most effective tool for bringing God's Spirit into my relationships. When I silently and repetitively pray to seek to love, comfort and understand, rather than to be loved, comforted and understood, before and during each human interaction, the effect is nothing short of magical. I become a channel for God's Spirit to flow into the encounter.

When I don't keep that prayer in mind, I revert to my default position. I automatically seek to BE loved, comforted and understood, and my selfishness blocks God's Spirit. Then, The Magic is absent and the door to conflict and misunderstanding is wide open.

I love you all.

March 14

Good morning.

Our keynote is "Honesty".

Today's Meditation and Prayer describe the power of perseverance.

There is something in me which regularly tells me I have performed so poorly and strayed so far from the Divine Spark that all is lost. I hear that voice of doom regarding large and small endeavors in both the material and spiritual realms. It insists I have strayed so far that there is no longer a next right action.

If I allow that lethal lie to control my actions, I am on a fast track to the abyss.

In truth, there is always a next right thing. I can't get far enough from my forgiving God's will that perseverance, coupled with God's grace and power, won't set me back on the right path.

Even though I can't envision it, if I persevere, The Magic will return.

For me, faith is persistently behaving correctly even when I think and feel it will do no good.

I love you all.

March 15

Good morning.

Our keynote is "Humbly say to ourselves many times today, 'Thy will be done'...".

In spiritual matters, today's Meditation and Prayer emphasize that we are only instruments; it's not up to us to figure out the future.

My ego rankles at the threat of my brain being dismissed from its CEO position.

Despite my ego's protests, my experience is that persistent, childlike reliance on Divine Guidance, one stitch at a time, works far better than struggling to execute my own grand plans.

When I revert to my default position of trying to figure out the patterns of my life so I will know where to start stitching, chaos is the usual result.

A chimpanzee has a better chance of mastering quantum physics than I have of foreseeing and comprehending the patterns of my life.

I am, however, responsible for, and have total power over, the actions which maintain my spiritual condition. I must take those actions in order to equip myself to hear and heed God's direction for the next stitch.

I find The Magic in stitching as a trusting little child and leaving all the patterns to the Master Planner.

I love you all.

March 16

Good morning.

Our keynote is: "Help God's kids do what they need to have done..."

The Meditation for the Day calls improving personal relationships our primary job. We are told to approach that effort with a singleness of purpose.

If we all adopted that angle of approach, most of the world's ills would evaporate.

I have found the Prayer of St. Francis to be a complete and almost infallible recipe for the improvement of personal relationships.

The Prayer asks that I may bring peace, love, forgiveness, harmony, truth, faith, hope, light, and joy to others while seeking to love, comfort, and understand them.

Offering the Prayer in the morning is of great benefit, but I find the real magic in silently praying to seek to love, comfort, and understand before and during every human encounter. Persisting in that approach has a magical effect on all my relationships and human interactions.

I love you all.

March 17

Good morning.

Our keynote is "Persistence".

Today's Meditation and Prayer tell us we do our best work when we are calm, but our usefulness is destroyed by emotional upset.

If I am to have a calm soul, I must, figuratively, clear the rattlesnakes from under my bed and refrain from putting more there.

No amount of prayer, meditation, meetings, or good works will stem the soul storms brought on by my dishonesty or other willful or persistent behavior contrary to God's will for me.

As my first sponsor taught, there is no way to become comfortable if I do things that eventually make me uncomfortable or fail to do things that will ultimately make me comfortable.

No exceptions, no barter.

While God's love for us is constant, it will not prevent persistent wrongdoing and/or procrastination from destroying my usefulness by blocking me from the magic of calmness.

I love you all.

March 18

Good morning.

Our keynote is "Courtesy".

The Thought for the Day emphasizes NOW as the only reality and the only time we can exercise any power.

The Meditation and Prayer mention "persistence" six times.

God didn't design me to be capable of perfection. Any progress I make is the result of persistence, often following failure, and sometimes in the face of fear and hopelessness.

Thinking about doing the right thing and resolving to persistently do so in the future feels good but accomplishes nothing. My intentions, thoughts, feelings, and beliefs never leave a footprint on reality.

Only my behavior has any impact beyond my mind.

I pray to act now on the knowledge that persistence is the key to The Magic.

Persistently seeking to do God's will in the right now often has a profound and beautiful impact on reality.

I love you all.

March 19

Good morning.

Our keynote is "Gratitude".

The Meditation for the Day promises us peace if we do our best to live according to God's plan for us and, thereby, are in harmony with the Holy Spirit.

I don't know God's overall plan for me.

The only glimpse of God's will I ever get is in the right now as the Divine Spark directs my single next stitch.

Happily, that is all the knowledge of God's will I need.

By persistently seeking to come as a little child and accepting the limitations of my understanding and power, I have experienced the promised peace. I also experience the implicit promise of soul turmoil and chaos when I lapse into pursuing my own will.

I cannot separate my spiritual well-being from my behavior.

Peace and harmony with God's Magic are less the result of how I am than of what I do.

I love you all.

March 20

Good morning.

Our keynote is "Humility."

The Meditation for the Day says even the actions we judge to be trivial may actually be of great importance. I am reminded of Gandhi's declaration that, even though all the things he had to do in a day were unimportant, it was of the utmost importance for him to do them.

The next right action (stitch), while looking insignificant to me, may prove crucial to God's plan. I have seen great blessings flow from seemingly mundane right actions. Unfortunately, I have also endured great chaos and negativity from my failure to do the right thing in matters which seemed clearly unimportant.

The results of heeding, or not heeding, God's guidance are far-reaching in both the spiritual and material realms. My job is to humbly take the next right stitch simply because it is right. God will assign its value and weave the results into The Magic.

I love you all.

March 21

Good morning.

Our keynote is "Honesty."

The Meditation for the Day discusses "wearing the world as a loose garment." It is described as not being upset about the surface wrongness of things but feeling deeply secure in faith that God is everything and all will work out according to God's plan.

The AA Big Book suggests that ultimately we all must choose between proceeding as if God is everything or as if God is nothing. If my perspective is that God is nothing, I am left with only the fleeting rewards and endless travails of this fickle world.

If given the opportunity to review our lives from the other side, I believe most of us will be appalled that we spent 99% of our time and energy on worldly pursuits which should not have been even 1% of our focus.

I pray not to forfeit my chance to consciously live in God's Magic today by behaving as if I believe God to be nothing.

I love you all.

March 22

Good morning.

Our keynote is: "Humbly say to ourselves many times today, 'Thy will be done'...".

Today's Meditation and Prayer emphasize that God is the source of all spiritual strength and power. We are further told that we grow spiritually primarily by helping other people.

It brings to mind a sentence in the AA Big Book which has profoundly enhanced my life: "The spiritual life is not a theory; we have to live it."

I find prayer, meditation, and some spiritual reading to be necessary. However, in my experience, those things are not really my spiritual life. Rather, they are merely preparation for the work with others which IS my spiritual life.

At any given moment, I believe my spirituality is measured by my behavior, rather than by my thoughts, feelings, or beliefs.

As always, I find The Magic through stitching as guided by the Divine Spark and focusing on others. There is no magic in thinking about and seeking to serve myself.

I love you all.

March 23

Good morning.

Our keynote is: "Pray to seek to love, comfort and understand...".

Today's Meditation suggests we should repeatedly say to ourselves, "All power is the Lord's," until negativity is driven from our minds and hearts.

It is precisely the process which is described more thoroughly in Emmett Fox's wonderful pamphlet, "The Golden Key," which is easily accessible online at no cost.

Fox's Golden Key is condensed to this: "Whatever the difficulty, if I can succeed in thinking about God instead of the difficulty, the difficulty will go away."

The Golden Key is only two pages long. It is not an essay to be read and studied but a simple blueprint for our actions. It tells us exactly how to accomplish thinking of God instead of the difficulty.

It has been my most helpful tool for overcoming problems and has magically helped me through hundreds of difficulties.

It must be used persistently, and the manner of the difficulties evaporating is often quite different than I had imagined. Nevertheless, it works. It really does!

I love you all.

March 24

Good morning.

Our keynote is: "Help God's kids do what they need to have done..."

Today's Meditation and Prayer emphasize how little we actually know. For me, they drive home the limit of my knowledge of God's will, as well as the limitation of my own power.

The fact is, the Divine Spark's guidance for my own very next action is the only glimpse of God's will I ever have. Often, I blur even that with my self-will and the crazy picture show in my head.

Likewise, my only real power is over my own next action. If I genuinely accept those limitations, a modicum of humility and a great deal of effectiveness may creep into my life.

God has, happily, set up the universe so that I don't need any more knowledge or power. If I prayerfully use my limited knowledge and abilities to take the next action as directed, God magically takes care of all things, both within and beyond my comprehension.

On my best, most productive days, it is clear to me that it all really is that simple.

I love you all.

March 25

Good morning.

Our keynote is "Persistence."

By serendipity, today's Meditation and Prayer are, like the keynote, devoted to persistence.

This double emphasis reminds me that, at times, I will feel like a total failure. On those occasions, a dark voice in me seeks to drive me into the abyss of giving up.

Many years ago, I had a conversation with a dry alcoholic who, for years, had successfully made his living playing poker. I asked him about any secrets of his success. He replied that ultimate success or failure at poker has little to do with the good hands. At the end of the day, he said, whether one succeeds or fails will depend on how the very worst hands are played.

I have found that observation to be valid in every area of life. Success has often come to me through persisting despite the voice of doom screaming the lie that I had failed beyond God's redemption.

Perfection is not on the menu for me. It is persistence, despite failures, which activates God's Magic.

I love you all.

March 26

Good morning.

Our keynote is "Courtesy."

Today's Meditation and Prayer declare that we must make the "venture of belief" by "crossing the bridge of faith."

When first exposed to AA, I took such statements to mean that I must change my mind and intellectually come to believe. For years, I tried in vain to directly alter my thoughts, feelings, and beliefs.

My journey to faith and belief finally began with the realization that a venture is very much action. One crosses a bridge by taking action, not by thinking themselves to the other side.

When I sought to behave, one stitch at a time, as one who has faith, I began, at once, to get the benefits that flow from faith.

In due course, the faithful action brought the comfort and joy of coming to believe and feeling that I am nestled in God's hands.

Today, when doubt resurfaces, if I continue to faithfully stitch, my actions will restore faith to my mind and soul.

I always find The Magic through my behavior, rather than the crazy picture show in my head.

I love you all.

March 27

Good morning.

Our keynote is "Gratitude."

The Meditation for the Day declares worldly wealth and power to have no permanence and to amount to very little in the end. I had always thought such ideas to be otherworldly and based on "You can't take it with you" or some hope of heaven.

My experience has proved, however, that trudging the spiritual path improves my here and now immensely. It's not just about the idea of an afterlife; it has turned out to be my only path to joy, peace, and usefulness in THIS world.

As a Divine Paradox, I seem to fare better in material matters when seeking to walk the spiritual path. When I focus on taking care of others, the universe seems to take care of me. Before sobriety, I spent most of my time and energy chasing the fool's gold of worldly acclaim and the myth of human security.

Today, I find The Magic by focusing on God and others. I lose it when I return to obsessing on myself and the things of this world.

I love you all.

March 28

Good morning.

Our keynote is "Humility."

Today's reading celebrates the miraculous transformation brought about by obedience in our "venture of faith." The idea of "obeying" still disturbs my ego.

However, in this context, it doesn't mean obeying other human beings or even all human rules. It merely means trying to take the next right action (stitch) as directed by conscience, moral compass, better angels, the Holy Spirit, or the Divine Spark. By any name, The Guide is the little piece of God which is in each of us.

Rejecting guidance of The Divine in the name of my intellect, dignity, or independence is the rankest form of self-will run riot and ultimately brings me chaos. Exactly to the extent I rebel against the Divine Spark, I abandon the venture of faith. In fact, today, obeying the Divine Spark, one stitch at a time, IS my venture of faith. If I am to live in God's Magic, I must obey my Creator as a little child obeys his or her parents.

I love you all.

March 29

Good morning.

Our keynote today is "Honesty," which happens to also be the theme of the 24 Hour Book's Thought for the Day. Early in sobriety, I was told that there are no degrees of honesty.

At any given time, I am either honest or dishonest. If I will be truthful UNLESS it is terribly costly, inconvenient, or embarrassing, I am simply dishonest.

I was also told that I am lying anytime I intend to cause a person to believe, or continue to believe, that a fact is different than I know it to be.

Perhaps most importantly, I have come to know that honesty without compassion is not really honesty. It is a form of hostility. I must carry, not just the truth, but the quiet, loving truth. Self-honesty is essential, but overthinking it can drive me into impotent self-obsession. Being honest with my fellows will move me toward self-honesty more effectively than mental gymnastics about self-honesty.

I know from painful experience that being dishonest will always block me from God's Magic.

I love you all.

March 30

Good morning.

Our keynote is: "Humbly say to ourselves many times today, 'Thy will be done'..."

Today's Meditation and Prayer suggest accepting criticism, as well as praise, and seeking not to be upset by the judgment of others.

That is a tall order for me because I am both wounded and frightened by criticism and negative judgment from others. However, my experience is that being judged by others is not as crippling as my own harsh and protracted judgment of myself. I must vigilantly guard against it, or I will cease positive action and fall into the abyss of hopelessness.

Frequently reminding myself that God's forgiveness is unlimited is very helpful. It is also useful to recall my first sponsor's frequent admonition that self-recrimination is the single most useless and counterproductive of all human endeavors.

Wallowing in regret and guilt never moves me a single stitch toward God's Magic. It just paralyzes me and destroys my ability to be useful to others.

I love you all.

March 31

Good morning.

Our keynote is: "Pray to seek to love, comfort, and understand..."

Today's Meditation and Prayer urge us to persevere (i.e., persist) in spite of our stumbling feet and to let God judge our progress.

I have found that angle of approach to be effective in both worldly and spiritual endeavors. I believe persistence in seeking to do God's will is pleasing to God, even when I feel I am stumbling too much to make real progress.

At some point in the process of achieving every significant success in my professional life, I have felt I was failing so miserably that it would be a disaster.

Likewise, any spiritual progress I have experienced has come from repeatedly stumbling a couple of steps in the right direction, being knocked over by self-will, saying "excuse me" to God, and stumbling another couple of steps in the right direction.

By persisting in that process, God's grace inches me closer to The Light. I usually can't see The Magic while I am persisting, but I surely see it as the result of persistence.

I love you all.

APRIL

April 1

Good morning.

Our keynote is: "Help God's kids do what they need to have done..."

Today's Meditation and Prayer affirm that we can do nothing of value without God's guidance. It reminds me of the mess I make of human relationships and everything else when I ignore the Divine Spark and try to arrange life to suit myself.

As my sponsor says, when trying to control events and people, I am like an ant floating down the river on a log, believing it is steering the log. Like such a deluded ant, I am running around frantically trying to control things beyond my power.

An enlightened ant would stop trying to be the pilot and simply take care of the little ant things that it CAN and should do. When I behave like a sensible and humble ant by accepting my limitations, my log drifts toward God's Magic. When I grab my imaginary rudder again, the ensuing chaos hides The Magic.

I love you all.

April 2

Good morning.

Our keynote is "Courtesy".

The Thought for the Day invites us to examine whether we have become better in the various roles God assigns us. Thoughtfulness in my human interactions is necessary. However, I must be careful not to overthink or attempt to script encounters. I am more useful and successful when I give my entire interest, attention, and love to one encounter at a time while BEHAVING like a good spouse, parent, friend, sponsor, lawyer, etc. as the situation requires.

When I feel inadequate in a role God has assigned, overexamination of myself has proved to be counterproductive. I get lost in obsession with how I am perceived. If I will lay aside fretting about what others think of me and persistently pray to seek to love, comfort, and understand others, something magic happens. My relationships are more peaceful and productive and are plagued by less conflict and misunderstanding.

Human relationships can seem humanly impossible, but bringing God and courtesy into them makes them easy.

I love you all.

April 3

Good morning.

Our keynote is "Persistence".

Today's Meditation reminds me that we are here on earth to serve others, and that is the beginning and the end of our real worth. I have come to believe that self-centeredness is the root of the wrongness and troubles of all humankind, not just alcoholics.

Looking back over my long life, I see clearly that the time and effort I devoted to trying to please myself has left very little of value. Almost everything of real, lasting worth has come as the result of trying to serve others and God by heeding the Divine Spark, one stitch at a time.

It is, once again, the Divine Paradox. The more I seek my own happiness and the love, comfort, and understanding of others, the more elusive those things become. The Magic is in losing myself in efforts to serve others and God. Only then do I find the happiness, love, comfort, and understanding I crave.

I love you all.

April 4

Good morning.

Our keynote is "Courtesy".

Today's Meditation stresses the "understand" part of seeking to love, comfort, and understand. I am sometimes guilty of praying to love, comfort, and understand and then not truly focusing on the person in front of me.

I need to take a genuine interest in what others say, do, think, feel, want, and need. Only by gaining some understanding of a person can I effectively offer them love and comfort. I need to keep in mind that giving effective love and comfort often requires a lot more listening than talking.

As Chuck C. said, giving my entire interest, attention, and love to someone makes them, for that moment, the most interesting thing in the world. That angle of approach is far more effective than half-listening while waiting impatiently to spout my canned wisdom.

The Magic is in thinking of others. It is never found by thinking about myself.

I love you all.

April 5

Good morning.

Our keynote is "Gratitude".

Today's Meditation and Prayer expand on yesterday's discussion of personal interactions and relationships. They implicitly affirm that human relations are often humanly impossible.

Trying to "figure out" how to make my dealings with others work to my satisfaction usually blows up in my face. I get far better results by not scripting conversations in advance, thinking of the other person instead of myself, and praying to love, comfort, and understand. In fact, silent repetition of the "...love, comfort, and understand" portion of the Prayer of St. Francis has been nothing short of magic in my human relations. It reverses my natural angle of approach, and I have never once had a human encounter go terribly when I have silently prayed it before and during the encounter.

It brings God into the situation, and God has spectacular people skills!

It works. It really does!

I love you all.

April 6

Good morning.

Our keynote is: "Honesty".

Today's reading encourages us to relinquish our hold on things of the world and receive them back from God.

When my angle of approach is that I possess MY house, MY family, MY money, MY car, MY reputation, etc., trying to protect and juggle it all becomes overwhelming.

On the other hand, if during my morning prayer and throughout the day, I accept and acknowledge that it all belongs to God, the weight of the world is lifted. I am then free to live and express my gratitude for having the gifts in my life just for the day.

Harboring the illusion that things, possessions, positions, and relationships belong to me makes a big deal of myself and wrings the joy out of life.

But being only God's steward for the day allows me to cherish the people, use and enjoy the things, and be a happy, joyous, and free magical creature in God's Magic World.

I love you all.

April 7

Good morning.

Our keynote is: "Humbly say to ourselves many times today, 'Thy will be done',..."

Today's Meditation and Prayer give us the antidote to the poison of self-obsession and dwelling on our troubles. We escape the abyss of self by turning our attention to others and how we can be helpful to them.

By nature, the first question popping into my mind about any situation or relationship is, "What am I getting out of this?" That question is a trap which ensures my dissatisfaction and continued self-obsession because the answer is always some form of "Not enough".

It is simply the wrong question

The Divine Paradox is that the only way for me to get true satisfaction from any situation or relationship is to approach it from the angle of, "What can I add to this? How can I be helpful?"

When I give my entire interest, attention, and love to the person or situation in front of me, obsession with myself and my difficulties magically fades away.

I love you all.

April 8

Good morning.

Our keynote is: "Pray to seek to love, comfort, and understand, ..."

According to the Thought for the Day, alcoholics attain faith by surrendering their lives to the God of their understanding.

I suspect all people who seek a life of faith must make a similar surrender.

When confronted with the choice between surrendering or dying, I thought I had to somehow change my thoughts, feelings, and beliefs, and then my behavior would follow.

I thought surrender was a mental process and, of course, was totally unable to accomplish it from that angle of approach.

The intellectual desire and intention to surrender my life had little effect until I began to behave, one stitch at a time, like one who had surrendered.

It turned out that the actions consistent with surrender ARE the surrender!

If I am to have a life of faith, I must persistently behave faithfully. I can't think, learn, or even pray my way into surrender or faith.

As always, The Magic is in the action, not the crazy picture show in my mind.

I love you all.

April 9

Good morning.

Our keynote is: "Help God's kids do what they need to have done..."

The Meditation for the Day declares our fears to be harmless phantoms, which we have dressed as monsters. Fear has been my greatest problem from my first memory through today. Unlike most alcoholics, fear has been bigger than resentment for me. I suspect I am too self-centered to give other people credit for having much impact on my life.

It has been helpful to view "fear" as an acronym for "False Events Appearing Real". Also, I am often comforted by Mark Twain's statement, "My life has been filled with many tragedies, almost none of which ever happened". The very essence of faith for me is taking the next right action despite my self-created terror. God never removes my fears while I fail to act.

I must pray and then at once begin positive action if I am to be relieved of fear and its attendant paralysis.

I love you all.

April 10

Good morning.

Our keynote is "Persistence".

The Meditation for the Day warns that God can only dwell in an obedient and humble heart. Pride is not called the first deadly sin by default. It is first because it is the most deadly. It vetoes obedience and humility and thereby blocks me from the Sunlight of the Spirit. Too much reliance on the human intellect and concern for myself sever my connection with the Divine Spark.

Without that connection, I am in charge and am destined to drive my life into chaos. Pride is insidious. It masquerades as responsibility, respectability, security, intelligence, common sense, and even spiritual superiority. Regardless of which mask it wears, the result is the same. It causes me to live in the darkness and futility of self-interest without awareness of God or God's Magic.

I love you all.

April 11

Good morning.

Our keynote is "Courtesy".

Of all the year's daily readings, today's theme of "discipline" may be the one I like the least and need the most. Lack of self-discipline and its Siamese twin, procrastination, have plagued me from my earliest memories. The AA Big Book says we alcoholics are undisciplined, but we allow God to discipline us in the simple way the book describes.

Only following that course has ever infused real, consistent discipline into my life. If I persistently seek to remain God conscious and heed the Divine Spark, one stitch at a time, miracles happen. While stitching as directed and persistently returning to the thought of God, my behavior becomes far more disciplined. It is never God's will for me to procrastinate.

Trudging that path, God makes me more useful, effective, comfortable, and free. Once more, God magically does for me what I cannot do for myself.

I love you all.

April 12

Good morning.

Our keynote is "Gratitude".

The Meditation for the Day declares an "expression of faith" to be all God needs to manifest Divine Power in our lives. But, what is an effective "expression of faith"? In my experience, it is not loudly proclaiming faith. Also, I have come to believe that the secure feeling we associate with faith is not really faith at all; it is the reward for faith. The feeling is marvelous but directly impacts nothing but me.

I believe I express my faith by persistently seeking to take the next action (stitch) as directed by the Divine Spark, especially when my brain and ego are screaming their vetoes. I have found effective faith to be expressed by action, not by words or my state of mind. When my behavior reflects the Divine Spark's triumph over my self-centered concerns, faith is quietly and effectively expressed. God's Magic is then in and around me.

I love you all.

April 13

Good morning.

Our keynote is "Humility".

Today's Meditation discusses making the world a better and happier place. In order for God to effectively use me to that end, I must persistently seek to do God's will a stitch at a time. Also, praying to seek to love, comfort, and understand before and during each human encounter gives me a much better chance of being gentle and loving. However, I have found nothing more effective than simply being persistently and universally courteous.

I have come to believe that courtesy is the most neglected and underrated of all spiritual attributes. Experience has convinced me that there is never a valid reason for discourtesy, and that "courteous" and "loving" are practically synonymous. In fact, I believe it is impossible for me to be either spiritual or loving while being discourteous. Courtesy is truly magic in human relations and indeed makes the world a better and happier place.

I love you all.

April 14

Good morning.

Our keynote is "Honesty".

Today's Meditation declares that balance in our lives can only be attained by keeping spirituality paramount.

I was sober several years before I was able to realize that truth. After becoming too busy with the gifts of sobriety, I spent years on a quest to balance my life. I used prayer, the steps, my sponsor, meetings, written inventories, and even outside counseling. Nevertheless, my life remained chaotic.

Finally, during a discussion meeting, I once again brought up my quest for balance. A young man, who was less than a week out of the asylum, responded, "Don, if you could balance your life, why couldn't you manage it?". Finally, I realized that balance and manageability are the same. I can no more balance my life than I can manage it. However, when I focus on God and heeding the Divine Spark, one stitch at a time, rather than intellectually seeking balance, a miracle happens. God magically balances and manages my life.

I love you all.

April 15

Good morning.

Our keynote is "Humbly say to ourselves many times today, 'Thy will be done'..."

The Meditation for the Day says we will accomplish more by remaining calm than by a long day of frantic activity. I have vainly sought calmness through alcohol, other drugs, psychology, and satisfaction of physical and material desires. Ironically, even sober, I have behaved frantically in my futile quest to quiet the turmoil. Merely trying to think and/or pray myself calm rarely works.

It is when I follow my prayers with maintaining God consciousness AND behaving calmly, one stitch at a time, that my "soul storms" pass. I am then more effective in helping others, and seeking to help them further soothes my soul. The magic is that, while I have no immediate control of my mind, God gives me power over my next action. As I exercise that power by behaving calmly and seeking to be helpful, my mind and soul are calmed.

I love you all.

April 16

Good morning.

Our keynote is "Pray to seek to love, comfort and understand..."

Today's Meditation and Prayer are devoted to "Love".

The Meditation for the Day tells us that love comes from thinking of every man or woman as our brother or sister. It would be ideal to perpetually maintain such perfect thoughts and feelings, but I cannot. Fortunately, I don't believe my thoughts and feelings determine whether or not I am loving.

I am loving when I behave lovingly and I am not loving when I do not behave lovingly. No exceptions. Regardless of the crazy picture show in my head, I can persistently treat everyone as my brother or sister. When my behavior is loving, I come into harmony with humankind and God. Then, and only then, I magically find myself thinking of everyone as my brother or sister and I feel the kinship. As a result of loving action, I both feel and receive love. Love that matters is action, not emotion.

I love you all.

April 17

Good morning.

Our keynote is "Help God's kids do what they need to have done..."

Today's reading is about strengthening our faith by persistently maintaining God consciousness and taking action consistent with faith.

It is necessary for me to use those tools regularly. Many times, I have been doubtful, frightened, weak, and despondent. Although I was certain it would do no good, I have taken to my knees and said a simple prayer of "please" and "thank you".

Then, while I am wrestling with my own demons, someone interrupts by bringing their pain to me. Initially, my heart sinks even further. I know I have nothing to give and, certainly, am too busy worrying about me to deal with the person. But if, instead of crawling deeper into myself, I silently and repetitively pray to love, comfort, and understand and give my entire interest, attention, and love to the person, the miracle happens one more time.

Doubt, fear, and self-obsession dissolve. Once more I am happy, joyous, and free in God's Magic. It works. It really does!

I love you all.

April 18

Good morning.

Our keynote is "Persistence".

Today's reading directs us to strive for friendliness and helpfulness. In order to have opportunities to be helpful, I believe it is crucial to communicate approachability with each gesture, expression, and word. People usually don't reach out for help to someone who is discourteous, surly, or radiates self-importance.

Nothing impacts our opportunities to be of service as greatly as whether people are comfortable approaching us. Practicing simple courtesy and praying, "Let me seek to love, comfort, and understand," draws people to us. Once someone does approach, I need to seek to give that person my entire interest, attention, and love. Unless someone senses that I'm really listening to them, nothing I say is likely to have much impact. The magic of being helpful is more often realized by listening and acting than by talking.

I love you all.

April 19

Good morning.

Our keynote is "Courtesy".

The Meditation for the Day promises that God will provide all the power we need as long as we persistently seek spiritual progress.

When I began to awaken to the necessity of pursuing a spiritual life, I envisioned it as steady, uninterrupted progress. The reality has proved to be very different. I get knocked off course by some form of self so frequently that it often feels as if I am making no progress.

However, by God's grace, after falling, I can get right back up, say a little "excuse me" prayer, and resume stitching as the Divine Spark directs until self blindsides me once again. This process often repeats itself many times a day.

Each time I fail, it feels as if my spiritual journey has been interrupted. However, the evidence is that persistence after failure, over and over, is my only route to spirituality and God's Magic. And, it turns out, stumbling and persisting along the path IS my spiritual life.

I love you all.

April 20

Good morning.

Our keynote is "Gratitude".

The Meditation for the Day discusses our power to choose between the right path and the wrong one. On the wrong path, I have no power for good, but by seeking to do God's will, I receive the power of God's Spirit. I can form an intention to walk the right path, but that intention has no reality until I start walking. My intentions don't become decisions until I act on them.

Ultimately, the only power I have to choose between right and wrong is in the right now for my very next action. The more "next right things" I do, the easier it is to continue to walk in the right direction. Conversely, the longer I ignore or defy Divine Guidance, the harder it is for me to break out of the downward spiral. Today, I pray to transform my intention to walk the right path into a decision, one step at a time. The magic is in walking the path, not thinking and talking about it.

I love you all.

April 21

Good morning.

Our keynote is "Humility".

The Meditation for the Day talks about "sin".

Before sobriety, no word rankled me more. Merely hearing it evoked a physical reaction. Shortly after getting sober, my allergy to hearing or reading the word was neutralized by my sponsor's explanation of its meaning in the original Greek language.

He said it is a term associated with archery and simply means "to miss the mark". Even in my rabid opposition to all things divine, I could live with the word by that definition.

For me, in this earthly life, "sin" now means failing to stitch as directed by the Divine Spark. When I persistently "miss the mark" without trying to correct my aim, it robs me of God's Magic and drives me into chaos and despair.

Today, I have an all-forgiving Higher Power who only requires that I say "excuse me" and promptly return to stitching in harmony with God's will.

Failure and persistent correction IS my spiritual life and is all God expects or requires from me.

I love you all.

April 22

Good morning.

Our keynote is "Humility".

The Thought for the Day emphasizes that it is not conversation or literature that ultimately convinces people that AA works or to otherwise seek a spiritual path. It is the silent message carried by the lives of those who have been miraculously lifted from the abyss.

I must strive to remember that each of us ALWAYS carries a message. If I am observed behaving selfishly, being discourteous, gossiping, failing to help others, or walking on the edge of dishonesty, it carries a clear message. That message is not likely to attract anyone to come to me for help or inspire them to seek recovery and/or a spiritual life. Such behavior will render my lip service to God and spirituality hollow and impotent.

On the other hand, if I am seen persistently trying to be helpful, courteous, and kind while seeking to heed the Divine Spark, someone may be moved to seek or be reinforced in seeking recovery and The Magic. My prayer is to remain aware of the message I carry throughout this day.

I love you all.

April 23

Good morning.

Our keynote is "Honesty".

Today's Meditation and Prayer emphasize the importance of conscious contact with God. Persistent thoughts of The Divine, we are told, will facilitate our cooperation with God.

Experience has convinced me that the key to a useful, sober, peaceful, successful life is cooperation with God, one stitch at a time. I believe acceptance of that truth is so difficult because of its simplicity. Our brains and egos reject the idea that all we need to do is maintain awareness of God and seek to heed the Divine Spark with our next action. That angle of approach doesn't make a sufficiently big deal of self to satisfy the ego.

It is deeply ingrained in us that the key to life is figuring out the patterns, envisioning the future, and making it happen through the exercise of our will and wits. That heady idea is so much a part of us that letting it go feels like a death of self.

Nevertheless, accepting the limitations of my vision and power by behaving, one stitch at a time, as a humble servant of God is the key to The Kingdom for me. I find The Magic only by coming as a little child.

I love you all.

April 24

Good morning.

Our keynote is: "Humbly say to ourselves many times today, 'Thy will be done',...".

Today's reading urges becoming more centered in God than in self and directing our will toward doing God's will.

I had many things backwards before sobriety. I believed relentless self-will and a drive to satisfy and enlarge self to be character assets. They turned out to be a one-way ticket to hell on earth.

Chuck C. believed all of life to be a struggle between the ego and God. I agree, and have long since accepted that my ego is never going to surrender. Each day, stitch after stitch, is a continuous stream of choices between God and self.

Whether I move upward towards the spiritual life or descend into the chaos and futility of self is not determined by my thoughts, feelings or beliefs. It depends completely on whether I persistently seek to take the next stitch in accordance with God's will or in my self-interest.

I don't find God's Magic with my brain. I find it with my feet.

I love you all.

April 25

Good morning.

Our keynote is: "Pray to seek to love, comfort and understand, ...".

The Meditation for the Day suggests saying "God bless him or her" when someone is in disharmony with us. It brings to mind both the Prayer of St. Francis and my first sponsor's admonition that a mud puddle never settles until someone stops stirring it.

Bringing harmony and peace to any negative situation by seeking to love, comfort and understand others is at the heart of the Prayer of St. Francis.

Regarding the "mud puddle", it was further emphasized that I never have the power to make the other person not start or to stop stirring it. Therefore, it is always my responsibility to not begin, or continue, to stir a mud puddle.

Turning the other cheek, instead of responding to venom with venom, removes my ego from a situation and brings God's Magic to it. As difficult as it often feels, responding to hatefulness with love and courtesy causes resentment, fear, anger and discord to fade away.

I love you all.

April 26

Good morning.

Our keynote is: "Help God's kids do what they need to have done,...".

The Meditation for the Day declares God's plan for our lives not to be ceaseless activity. God's Power, it continues, is available when we seek to do God's will, but never when we are trying to arrange life to suit ourselves.

Often, I have seen more accomplished in a few minutes of prayerful, God and other centered action than an entire day of frantic, self-centered activity.

Experience has taught me the difference between action and activity. Action is seeking Divine Guidance for each stitch while focusing on others and God. Activity is focusing on myself and being driven by ego and self-will.

Action magically expands time and energy and makes me helpful, effective, joyful and peaceful.

Activity is ultimately futile and often counterproductive. It drains energy, obscures the Divine Spark, sows disharmony and casts my mind and soul into confusion and chaos.

There is no magic in the fool's errand of self-will run riot.

I love you all.

April 27

Good morning.

Our keynote is "Perseverance".

Today's reading discusses our inability to directly see God and concludes that we must perceive the Divine by spiritual perception or vision.

In my experience, whether or not I perceive God at any given time depends on which pair of glasses I choose to wear.

Some days I take my fellow humans, the grandeur of nature, and the fact that I am a sober, living human being for granted.

Through that pair of glasses it all looks rather commonplace and often tiresome or frightening. I don't see or feel God's Magic World.

However, by choosing a different pair of glasses, I can see the magic of nature, sobriety, and life itself.

I can be aware that my fellows are the only tangible part of God I can see or with which I can interact.

Through those spectacles, anytime I see or feel love, I am seeing and feeling God.

I pray not to squander the gift of this day by walking through it blind to God's presence in my fellows, the world, and myself.

I love you all.

April 28

Good morning.

Our keynote is "Courtesy".

Today's Meditation and Prayer declare maintaining God consciousness and helping others to be our proper missions. Either of those endeavors is a powerful force for good. I can provide some help to others even though I am not immediately conscious of God. Also, I can enjoy consciousness of God for a little while when not actively seeking to be helpful.

However, when I merge those two divine objectives, they enhance one another remarkably. Divine consciousness motivates and equips me to be more useful to my fellows. Likewise, helping others greatly facilitates my awareness of God. Practiced together, God consciousness and helpfulness to my fellows can rocket me into God's Magic (i.e., a fourth dimension of existence)!

I love you all.

April 29

Good morning.

Our keynote is "Gratitude".

The Thought and Prayer for the Day expand on yesterday's theme by discussing harmony with God and humankind. It is difficult to maintain harmony with my fellows when I am not aware of God, or my behavior is contrary to God's will. Likewise, I cannot be in harmony with God while I am resentful of, dishonest with, or discourteous toward my fellows.

Being in harmony with both God and others is the most useful, comfortable, loving, and effective state of being for me. Maintaining conscious contact with God is the first step toward harmony with The Divine. When I couple God consciousness with behaving as one who seeks to love, comfort, and understand others, I will be courteous, forgiving, and helpful to all. As a result of that partnership of God's power and grace with my faithful, loving actions, God's Magic will fill and surround me.

I love you all.

April 30

Good morning.

Our keynote is "Honesty".

Today's reading discusses the Divine Spark, which is God's presence within each of us. If developed and heeded, it will guide my actions, one stitch at a time. The Spark is called by many names, including conscience, moral compass, better angels, and the Holy Spirit. It responds to exercise, or the lack of it, precisely like our bodies. When I focus on The Spark and try to stitch as directed, it grows in strength and definition. It is strengthened by prayer, maintenance of God consciousness, honesty, courtesy, and seeking to help others.

Each selfless act to the benefit of my fellows strengthens my connection with The Divine. However, when persistently ignored or spurned, the Spark atrophies until It is no longer a factor, and then I am truly lost. The Divine Spark is my guide to The Magic. I pray to behave in a manner that will keep its signal strong and clear.

I love you all.

MAY

May 1

Good morning.

Our keynote is "Humbly say to ourselves many times today, 'Thy will be done'..."

The Thought for the Day defines "charity" as caring enough about others to really want to help them. Alcoholics, if they are to live sober and comfortably, must practice charity by carrying the message of recovery to suffering alcoholics. However, the necessity of acting charitably is not confined to alcoholics.

My experience convinces me that it is essential for anyone who seeks to live a useful, peaceful, and abundant life. Perhaps my all-time favorite quote is from the renowned psychiatrist, Alfred Adler. It is addressed to a patient as follows: "You can be healed of depression if every day you begin the first thing in the morning to consider how you can bring a real joy to someone else. If you can stick to this for two weeks, you will no longer need therapy; you will no longer be depressed." That is magic indeed!

I love you all.

May 2

Good morning.

Our keynote is "Pray to seek to love, comfort, and understand..."

Today's Meditation declares that we must BE before we can DO. On the surface, that statement may seem to contradict the message that action is the heart of it all. However, I believe it to be perfectly consistent.

We must BE willing to prepare ourselves to be helpful by DOING things to enhance and maintain our spiritual condition. As with all of life, that is given reality by taking one stitch after another as directed by the Divine Spark. Sometimes, the next right stitch is to pray, read, meditate, go to a meeting, or otherwise seek to enlarge and maintain spirituality. Then I AM prepared to be helpful.

We are then presented with opportunities to DO helpful things when God knows we are prepared, not when we think we are ready. And, each time God puts us in a position to be useful and we seek to DO so, we, magically, will BE better prepared to respond to the next opportunity. We must be to do, but we also must do to be.

I love you all.

May 3

Good morning.

Our keynote is "Help God's kids do what they need to have done".

Today's reading discusses forgiveness. We are told that we must overcome ourselves before we can truly forgive others.

My belief and experience are that self can only be overcome by persistently seeking to behave better than I think, feel, and believe. The steps, prayer, meditation, meetings, etc., are necessary preparation. However, for them to have a real impact, I must cease to require that I feel forgiving in order to behave forgivingly.

The Lord's Prayer asks God to forgive me precisely in the manner and to the extent I forgive others. If I act out forgiveness to my fellows, regardless of the old crazy picture show in my head, and God does the same for me, I am fine.

I don't really need God to feel forgivingly toward me, but I desperately need God to act forgivingly! Behaving forgivingly before I feel it IS the overcoming of myself. It magically brings the peace of feeling forgiveness.

I love you all.

May 4

Good morning.

Our keynote is "Persistence".

The Thought for the Day reminds me of the overwhelming power of my ego.

Before sobriety, I went to ridiculous extremes trying to make myself appear smart, successful, rich, etc.

Unfortunately, I am not immune to that inclination in sobriety.

My lifelong ego disorder makes me, without divine intervention, an egomaniac with an inferiority complex.

Without spiritual help, I will feel too good for someone or something and, at the same instant, know I am not nearly good enough for that same person or thing.

The obsession with how I feel and how I compare to others has been the root of most of my troubles.

AA's 12 steps and fellowship, seeking to behave as the Divine Spark directs and turning my attention to others, have proved to be the only effective tools to counter my riotous ego.

Magically, embracing and using those tools quiets the crazy picture show in my head and allows me to be neither above nor below God's other children.

Only then can I be a fellow among fellows, comfortable with both others and myself.

I love you all.

May 5

Good morning.

Our keynote is: "Courtesy".

The Meditation for the Day emphasizes that we cannot realize spirituality through our intellect.

The Scriptures similarly caution against leaning too much on our own understanding.

Trying to use my limited human intellect to realize the infinite and divine is a vanity which leads only to more questions and confusion. A monkey is more likely to master quantum physics than I am to find and comprehend God with my intellect.

However, if I approach spirituality like a little child and behave faithfully by heeding the Divine Spark, one stitch at a time, it results in a visceral certainty that I am cradled in the loving hands of God.

It is good news that I realize God's Magic through my behavior, which I can control, rather than through my immediately uncontrollable mind.

I love you all.

May 6

Good morning.

Our keynote is "Gratitude".

Today's Meditation and Prayer declare spirituality to be the only cure for the weariness which permeates today's world.

In essence, the Meditation tells us that the cause of world weariness is self-centeredness.

I absolutely agree. Nothing wears me down and hinders my connection with God and my fellows like continuously thinking about me. When chronically focusing on myself, I am certain to become weary, and then can carry only weariness to those around me.

However, when I maintain God consciousness and seek to give my entire interest, attention, and love to others, I am less consumed by self.

When I couple that approach with repetitive silent prayers to seek to love, comfort, and understand my fellows, rather than seeking the same from them, I further benefit from God's Magic. I then have a chance to be a tiny part of the antidote for world weariness rather than a carrier of it.

I love you all.

May 7

Good morning.

Our keynote is "Humility".

The Meditation for the Day calls the combination of our faithful efforts and God's direction the "recipe for spiritual success".

I sometimes view my life as if it were a construction project.

God is the architect, I am the simple laborer, and the Divine Spark's guidance is the blueprint.

The greatest architectural plans come to naught unless someone starts building. On the other hand, a simple laborer cannot create a cathedral unless there is an overall plan and he or she heeds specific guidance.

Magically, if each laborer performs one task at a time as directed, the structure, which was conceived in the mind of the architect, comes into reality.

Put another way, any spiritual success in my life comes from my employer/employee type relationship with God.

Following the boss's orders, as conveyed through the Divine Spark, one stitch at a time, will produce beauty, usefulness, and success far beyond my imagination.

I love you all.

May 8

Good morning.

Our keynote is "Honesty".

Today's Meditation and Prayer urge us to go slowly and calmly from task to task (i.e., stitch to stitch).

I need that reminder every day. Hurrying is so ingrained in me that my default position is to hurry even when there is no need to do so.

The overwhelming majority of things I botch and regret happen while I am in a rush.

My frantic activity flows from making a big deal of my tasks, and, thereby, of myself.

It is difficult for me to be conscious of God while going at a breakneck pace. I am much less likely to lapse into rushing when I am conscious of God and view myself and my tasks as little deals.

My most efficient, effective, and useful work magically happens when I focus on God and others rather than obsessing on myself and the work.

Calmly and prayerfully giving unhurried attention to my tasks yields far better results than treating them as big deals.

It is another Divine Paradox.

I love you all.

May 9

Good morning.

Our keynote is "Humbly say to ourselves many times today, 'Thy will be done'...".

Today's Meditation and Prayer emphasize reliance on God in human relationships.

I have found human relationships to be ultimately humanly impossible. However, they unfold smoothly with God present as the Divine Third.

I cannot overstate the value of praying, "Let me seek to love, comfort, and understand," before and during my human interactions. It changes everything.

When I relapse into concern with how I sound and whether people are going to love, comfort, and understand me satisfactorily, my relationships jump the track every time.

I can always tell I am moving in the wrong direction when I start scripting future conversations so they will turn out the way I want.

Today, I pray to let God's Magic work in all my interactions with God's other children.

I love you all.

May 10

Good morning.

Our keynote is "Pray to seek to love, comfort, and understand...".

The Meditation for the Day bluntly states, "Calmness is constructive of good. Agitation is destructive of good".

Amen.

I seek to adopt the objective of my late friend, Sandy B., to always be the least disturbed person in the room.

When I am extremely emotionally upset, there is no consciousness of God, and a lunatic is in control of my life.

I am living in my "big deals", which means I have made a big deal of myself. When doing so, I am disconnected from God, bereft of genuine love, and stripped of efficiency.

There is no greater thief of my peace than "big deals", good or bad. They are synonymous with stress, which always eradicates peace and can destroy me. My "big dealism" can be fatal.

I pray today to have only little bitty deals and allow myself to be filled and surrounded by the Magic of God's perfect peace and calm.

I love you all.

May 11

Good morning.

Our keynote is "Help God's kids do what they need to have done...".

Today's Meditation and Prayer again emphasize that personal relationships cannot be entirely right without the presence of God's Spirit.

That affirms my belief and experience that it is only by the inclusion of God/Love that human relations are filled with lasting peace and joy.

One of the keys to my coming to believe in God at all was the realization that if God is Love, then Love is God.

So, when I bring God into a relationship, Love is present. Likewise, even if I am not actively thinking of God, when I bring real unselfish Love to my human encounters, God is present.

The presence of God/Love overcomes the human ego's obstacles and booby traps and enables peaceful, joyful, and lasting relationships.

Praying to seek to love, comfort, and understand others summons the Divine Third and brings God's Magic into my human interactions.

I love you all.

May 12

Good morning.

Our keynote is "Persistence".

Today's reading cautions us to shield our minds from doubt, fear, and resentment. Such thoughts and feelings can and will, if persistently harbored, steal my faith, courage, and love, which are far more precious than any material possessions.

Negative thoughts and feelings come to me uninvited and unwanted and then try to take over my soul. My protection must come from positive action and consciousness of God. Any positive action helps drive away negativity, but seeking to help another human being is most effective of all.

Actions that help me maintain or regain my God consciousness include prayer, meditation, and using Emmett Fox's wonderful Golden Key. Simple reminders to think of God, such as a rubber band around my wrist, a crumbled note in my pocket, or holding the door for God just a fleeting instant before entering a room or car, facilitate my awareness of God. By doing so, they provide much-needed spiritual armor.

If I persistently practice the presence of God, The Magic will eventually triumph over the inner forces that would destroy me.

I love you all.

May 13

Good morning.

Our keynote is "Courtesy".

Today's Meditation and Prayer urge us not to judge others. My first sponsor explained that I would know if God wanted me to be a judge because I would have a robe and a gavel. In the absence of those indicators of judicial status, he highly recommended that I refrain from judging.

In early sobriety, I was highly judgmental of myself because it seemed I was constantly judging. Just walking down the street, my brain would judge (usually harshly) almost every stranger passing by.

I have always been and remain unable to consistently control what rolls through the crazy picture show in my head.

It was a great relief to realize that unbidden and fleeting thoughts do not make me judgmental. I am not judgmental unless or until I behave or speak judgmentally.

No one is hurt by the old crazy picture show in my head. It never leaves a footprint on reality UNLESS I allow it to dictate my behavior.

Magically, the longer I refrain from behaving or speaking judgmentally, the fewer judgmental thoughts I have.

I love you all.

May 14

Good morning.

Our keynote is "Gratitude".

The Thought for the Day describes some benefits of the AA way of life and spirituality in general. One of those benefits is relief from our troubles and worries through a new way of looking at things.

That positive view of life is what Chuck C. called a "New Pair of Glasses".

I have a choice of "glasses" each day. I can view the universe as a hostile place in which I must try to wrest my needs and wants from its stingy and unwilling grip. That is a lonely and terrifying place in which I am dependent upon my own woefully inadequate wit and guile.

Or, I can choose to view myself as a magical creature living in God's Magic World where my purpose is to be helpful to God's kids, and God, in turn, will take care of me. In that world, a loving God provides all my needs unless I block The Grace by my selfishness.

In a very real way, my choice of "glasses" for the day determines whether I live that day in heaven or in hell.

I love you all.

May 15

Good morning.

Our keynote is "Humility".

Today's Meditation and Prayer encourage us to seek the spiritual before the material.

The Big Book validates that guidance by telling us that material well-being always follows spiritual growth; it is never the other way around.

My original sponsor viewed material things as inherently neither good nor bad but spiritually neutral. However, he continued, love of the world and prioritizing it over the spiritual is certain to result in futility and soul-sickness.

Looking back, I can see the ultimate triviality of material things and worldly success which seemed so important at times.

Everything good and lasting in my life, magically, comes from God as a byproduct of seeking to heed the Divine Spark and be of use to my fellows.

I believe there is a God-shaped hole in each of us that can never be filled by any combination of worldly goods and success.

I love you all.

May 16

Good morning.

Our keynote is "Honesty".

The Prayer for the Day asks that I may form the habit of daily prayer. I tend to form habits easily and let go of them reluctantly, if at all. That trait was a major factor in the total destruction of my life. However, God has taken that near-lethal flaw and turned it into one of the foundations of my sober life.

In 1981, I reluctantly began to get on my knees morning and night to ask and thank something I doubted was there. It became a habit and grew into, more or less, an obsession. In the thousands of days since April of 1981, I could count on my fingers the missed days of kneeling to pray. As a result of those prayers and other actions consistent with faith, I came to believe, and faith found me.

By persistent action, I also formed habits of going to meetings, doing and living the steps, helping others, etc. Those habits saved my life in 1981 and remain at the heart of my sober life today. If I persist in faithful behavior, God magically uses even my erstwhile flaws for good!

I love you all.

May 17

Good morning.

Our keynote is: "Humbly say to ourselves many times today, 'Thy will be done'...".

The Thought for the Day references the biblical story of the Good Samaritan who stopped and rendered aid to a stranger who had been robbed and beaten.

I suspect the situation did not look appealing, and the Samaritan must have known that he was volunteering for complications. At the very least, it was going to be a massive inconvenience.

The story reminds me that there is limited spiritual value in helping people I like and want to help. The greater spiritual reward comes when I must overcome my desire to cross the road and leave the wounded person for someone else to help. Under those circumstances, I am truly giving to the person in need instead of seeking to make myself feel better by doing what I wanted to do anyway.

I pray to seek to be helpful anytime God puts a needy brother or sister in my path, not just when I find it pleasant and convenient. The greatest magic is in doing the right thing when I really do not want to do it.

I love you all.

May 18

Good morning.

Our keynote is: "Pray to seek to love, comfort and understand...".

The Thought for the Day emphasizes the necessity of AA members seeking to help others if they are to be comfortably sober. AA didn't discover the spiritual law underlying that requirement. Helping others has always been necessary for anyone who would live a joyful, peaceful, and successful life.

I was told by my first sponsor that selfishness and self-centeredness, which is the root of our alcoholism, is not peculiar to alcoholics but is the malady of humankind. With alcoholics, it is particularly lethal due to our physical allergy to, and mental obsession with, alcohol.

Seeking to serve only my own needs and desires simply does not work. It ultimately results in discord, isolation, misery, and chaos. On the other hand, seeking to love, comfort, and understand others has a magical effect on me as well as my human encounters and relationships. It works its magic every time I lay aside self-concern and return to thinking of, and seeking to be helpful to, God's other kids.

I love you all.

May 19

Good morning.

Our keynote is "Help God's kids do what they need to have done..."

The Thought for the Day emphasizes the importance of fellowship.

There are many benefits of spiritual fellowship, in and out of AA, but one in particular comes to mind.

My insane ideas never introduce themselves by saying, "Good morning, Don. I'm a crazy idea and I'm here to try to kill you."

Instead, they tend to present as common sense, telling me things like, "It won't do any REAL harm," "Nobody will know," or "You are only going to do it once."

The disorder of my perception makes me vulnerable to putting my sobriety and entire life at risk by believing and acting on such poisonous self-deception.

Part of the fellowship's Magic is that my insane ideas never sound like common sense to you, and yours never sound like common sense to me.

My mind is like a bad neighborhood; I shouldn't go in there alone.

I love you all.

May 20

Good morning.

Our keynote is "Persistence".

The Thought for the Day tells us that being of service is one of the finest experiences one can have and will make us feel better.

I love and need time when my phone is uncharacteristically quiet and I have time to just be alone with my wife, my cats, and myself.

But often my precious respite is interrupted by a call from, or regarding, someone in need of support and help. My selfishness tells me that I need and deserve my rest and someone else can help this one.

However, by the grace of God, I usually behave better than I feel and think. Rather than curling back into my own comfort, I respond by saying something like, "I'm glad you called. What can I do to be helpful?"

Then a miracle happens. My selfish reluctance is replaced by an energy, joy, and love far superior to enjoying my "me time".

From my experience, I can affirm that today's reading states truth.

It works. It really does!

The joy which flows from having sacrificed what I want to do in order to seek to be helpful to another human being is unsurpassed.

It is The Magic!

I love you all.

May 21

Good morning.

Our keynote is "Courtesy".

Today's Meditation and Prayer warn against praying and talking spirituality but failing to take the appropriate action.

An example that has long resonated with me is "the toothache".

The only way I have found to turn a toothache over to God is by going to a dentist.

Prayer, going to meetings, and consulting my sponsor provide zero relief unless followed by the action necessary to place myself in a dentist's chair.

Without prayer, my frantic activity will usually prove fruitless and often be counterproductive.

Conversely, if I pray but fail to do the required footwork, my prayers generally come to naught.

The Magic appears only when my plea for God's grace and power is coupled with persistently stitching as directed by the Divine Spark.

I love you all.

May 22

Good morning.

Our keynote is "Gratitude."

Today's reading counsels that as children of God, we are entitled to claim God's strength.

In early sobriety, I was taught that God has an infinite supply of power, life, health, love, money, etc., and wants to shower us with those blessings.

I am blocked from God's bounty only by my ego, my fear, and the mirage of self-reliance.

If I am concerned primarily with myself and taking care of me, I am terrified of scarcity and never feel I have enough. I am dependent on my own poor human resources in trying to wrest what I need or want from the unwilling grip of a hostile universe.

But if I focus on God and helping others, all God's strength and plenty are mine.

For today, I pray to behave as one who lives in the magic of God's bounty instead of in the spiritual poverty, despair, and fear of self-reliance.

I love you all.

May 23

Good morning.

Our keynote is "Humility."

The Prayer for the Day asks that I may leave the outcome of my actions to God and seek no credit for the results of what I do. It is powerful and directly on point with today's keynote.

In leaving the outcome to God, I accept the absolute limitation of my power to only my very next action.

I also accept that my knowledge of God's will never goes further than my own next stitch.

If I take no credit for positive outcomes of my actions, I am also free from self-recrimination when my efforts fail to produce the desired results.

When employing that angle of approach, I am not crushed and hobbled by making a big deal out of myself, regardless of the results of my efforts.

Magically, God then makes me more efficient, effective, useful, and peaceful.

I love you all.

May 24

Good morning.

Our keynote is "Honesty."

Today's Meditation declares that the more of God's strength we give away, the more we will keep. On the negative side, it also promises that we will ultimately lose that which we try to hoard for ourselves.

In AA, we often hear, "In order to keep it, we must give it away."

I have come to believe that giving is even more important; in order to truly GET it, we have to give it away.

Of course, we can't give that which we do not have.

However, when we seek to help others with what we DO have, our own reserves magically expand. We are taken to new levels of love, peace, and usefulness.

With each selfless act of giving, we are drawn closer to God and our fellows while our own souls are fed. Therefore, the next time we seek to give "it" away, we will have more to give.

I love you all.

May 25

Good morning.

Our keynote is: "Humbly say to ourselves many times today, 'Thy will be done',...'"

Today's Meditation and Prayer urge us to continue trying to help others, even when we feel spiritually empty and/or it seems no one is responding.

With regard to the latter, thank goodness the 12th Step of AA directs us to CARRY the message, not DELIVER it. Delivery is beyond my control; it is up to God and the other person.

My job is the quiet, loving presentation of the truth. It is useless and often counterproductive to fret, browbeat, and manipulate trying to make sure the person "gets" it. If I take credit for those who heed the message and blame for those who do not, I make working with others so difficult that I can accomplish little.

The Magic is in realizing the limitations of my power and not making a big deal of me or my role. That angle of approach frees me to do a much better job of what I CAN do, rather than squandering energy on what I cannot do.

I love you all.

May 26

Good morning.

Our keynote is: "Pray to seek to love, comfort, and understand...".

Today's Meditation and Prayer return to an uncomfortable subject on which I sorely need daily help, "self-discipline". Lack of that quality has produced more fear, failure, embarrassment, and guilt than any of my other shortcomings. I have spent untold hours trying, in vain, to figure out why I fall short and how I can better discipline myself. However, my only real progress has come from the simple solution offered by the AA Big Book. It directs me to accept that I am undisciplined, maintain God consciousness, and allow God to discipline me, one stitch at a time. When I humbly say to myself many times each day, "Thy will be done", and seek to persistently stitch as the Divine Spark directs, something magical happens. My life begins to vaguely resemble that of a person who has a smattering of self-discipline!

I love you all.

May 27

Good morning.

Our keynote is: "Pray to seek to love, comfort, and understand...".

The Prayer for the Day asks that my life be rooted in faith and for me to feel deeply secure.

Most of us spend much of our lives in quest of human security. Having devoted decades to that quest, I have found it to be a fool's errand. All the world's riches and acclaim cannot assure my next breath, expel my fear, or fill the emptiness in my soul. Security, based on material and human things, is a myth. It does not exist. The only real security I can ever know must be based on faith in God and behaving as directed by the Divine Spark.

It is ironic and magical that security does not come from what I can see and touch. It must be based on the unseen. Nothing but God will fill the God-shaped hole in my soul and allow me to feel deeply secure.

I love you all.

May 28

Good morning.

Our keynote is: "Help God's kids do what they need to have done...".

Today's reading encourages us to "...practice the presence of God".

To that end, AA's 11th step suggests prayer and meditation each morning and night. However, those exercises consume no more than 5% of my day. It is between the morning and evening prayer and meditation when I am most prone to forget all about God.

Fortunately, the Big Book gives clear directions for practicing the 11th Step all day long. We are directed to pause when agitated or doubtful and ask for the right thought or action. It continues by telling us to constantly remind ourselves that we are no longer running the show and humbly say to ourselves many times each day, "Thy will be done".

When thus persistently practicing the presence of God, we are promised to magically "...be in much less danger of excitement, fear, anger, worry, self-pity, or foolish decisions". We are further promised we will become much more efficient.

It is the persistent all-day practice of the presence of God which blesses us with those beautiful and practical 11th Step Promises.

I love you all.

May 29

Good morning.

Our keynote is "Persistence".

Today's Thought, Meditation, and Prayer are all about seeking to be God's instrument in lightening the burdens of our fellows.

It usually doesn't just happen that we are put in a position to help many people with their burdens. If I am to have opportunities to be helpful, I must first seek to be courteous, kind, and attentive to every person I encounter. If my actions, words, and demeanor carry a message of light and hope, it invites people to bring their burdens to me.

But if I am lost in my own personal concerns, I will not appear approachable and am likely to be left alone in my self-obsession. I will not experience the magic that comes from thinking of and doing for others rather than myself.

Today, I pray to behave in a manner that will encourage others to approach and share their burdens with me.

I love you all.

May 30

Good morning.

Our keynote is "Courtesy".

Today's Meditation and Prayer are devoted to gratitude and humility.

Daily I try to work the word "magic" into these comments. I am referring to God, the source of all magic; certainly not the occult or stage illusions. I use the word to foster gratitude and humility and to counter my appalling capacity for taking the greatest gift in the universe for granted.

I love the story of a man who was obsessed with whether there really is magic in the world. After an epic quest, a wise person told him, "My son, it is all magic."

That I am a living, sober human being on this day, out of all the billions of days that have passed and will come to pass without me, is truly Magic!

It is statistically less likely than winning Powerball. With that in mind, the way the gift is wrapped doesn't matter much.

Awareness of the magnitude of God's gift of life this day makes it easier to be humble, grateful, joyous, and useful.

I love you all.

May 31

Good morning.

Our keynote is "Gratitude".

Today's reading discusses the nature and benefits of prayer.

A little over 41 years ago, at the insistence of my new AA mentors, and despite my reluctance and total skepticism, I began to pray on my knees every morning and night.

The miracles flowing from following those directions include staying sober and coming to believe. As I began to realize the value of prayer, I became concerned about the wording in my prayers and often not "feeling" right. When I took those concerns to my sponsor, he explained that there is nothing intellectual or psychological about prayer; God needs no information or special wording from me.

The only thing of real value, he said, is to come as a little child and humble myself before my Creator to say "Please" and "Thank you".

Despite my doubts, wandering mind, and my prayers often not "feeling" right, persistently praying on my knees has worked like magic every day for 41 years.

I love you all.

JUNE

June 1

Good morning.

Our keynote is "Humility".

Today's reading again urges us to seek and maintain God consciousness. We are promised that doing so, coupled with seeking to do God's will, one stitch at a time, will actually transform us.

Employing that angle of approach leads me to periods of feeling securely nestled in God's loving hands. At those times, doing the next right thing feels intuitive and becomes relatively easy. Then I am doing the right thing because I want to and finally know true freedom.

However, my experience is that I can only visit that fourth dimension of existence. I can't permanently reside there. I still regularly lose conscious contact with God and have to begin again.

Despite my stumbling feet, if I persist in starting over, I indeed become a different and better person. Persistence regularly transports me back to the joy and security of God's Magic from the hard scrabble world of self.

I love you all.

June 2

Good morning.

Our keynote is "Honesty".

Today's Meditation contains the perfect mission statement for living. The goal of life, it declares, is the gradual elimination of selfishness by the growth of love for God and our fellow human beings.

Such growth doesn't come from learning about, or even feeling, love. It flows from one single loving action followed by another.

We are told that persistence in those loving actions will result in a faint resemblance to the Divine Love. Perhaps, it is that faint likeness which is so attractive to AA newcomers and the world at large.

Magically, the more loving actions we do, the more opportunities we are given to do them.

Often, the greatest gift we can give earthly parents is to shower loving care on their children. I am convinced that the greatest (and maybe only) gift I can offer God is my loving care of God's other children.

I love you all.

June 3

Good morning.

Our keynote is: "Humbly say to ourselves many times today, 'Thy will be done'...".

Today's Meditation and Prayer urge us to love all people and God. I don't believe they are suggesting that we can always harbor the warm, pleasant feeling which we call love.

In my experience, feeling love is often the reward for the sometimes hard work of DOING love to others and to God.

There is limited spiritual value in doing loving and faithful things when it is what I want to do.

My hardest and most spiritually valuable love of others is behaving lovingly toward those I find unlovable and unappreciative at the most inconvenient times.

Similarly, the greatest fertilizer of my faith is behaving as one who has faith in God when my feeling of faith is at its lowest ebb.

I often experience the magical feelings of love and faith as a result of behaving more lovingly and faithfully than I feel.

I love you all.

June 4

Good morning.

Our keynote is: "Pray to seek to love, comfort, and understand..."

As per today's Meditation, that which is of this world is only the clay with which we are to mold something spiritual.

Consistent with today's message, I was taught that material things are spiritually neutral; inherently neither good nor bad. Whether they are spiritual assets or liabilities is determined by the way I view and use them.

When I perceive things, relationships, and reputation as belonging to me and being for my gratification, security, etc., there is never enough. I live in fear of losing them or not getting more. I turn them into a constant burden by hoarding them to myself.

It is very different when I see them as blessings, on day to day loan from God, for my use in helping my fellows and in doing God's will. They are then joyous and useful, and I am not enslaved to them.

There is no magic in having what is MINE, but there is great magic in the proper stewardship of God's gifts.

I love you all.

June 5

Good morning.

Our keynote is: "Help God's kids do what they need to have done..."

Today's Meditation and Prayer discuss the part of each human being which is of God and is available to guide our actions.

It is called many things, including moral compass, conscience, Divine Voice, Holy Spirit, etc. I call it the Divine Spark.

By any name, if I cultivate and obey The Spark, one stitch at a time, I become a conscious part of God's Magic. It leads me into harmony with my fellows, God, and the universe. I become useful, effective, and peaceful and am awash in God's bounty.

However, if I either ignore the Spark or defiantly refuse to follow Its direction, It fades from my awareness. Then, I am rudderless in a hostile universe, desperately trying to wrest my needs and wants from its unwilling grasp.

Today, I pray to revere, nourish, and obey the inner bit of my Creator which lights my path, one step at a time.

I love you all.

June 6

Good morning.

Our keynote is: "Persistence".

Today's reading emphasizes the sufficiency of God for all our needs at all times.

Whatever and wherever we need God to be, God will be. It brings to mind the following powerful assertion from AA's Big Book: "Either God is everything or God is nothing".

Today, I pray to renew my acceptance of God as everything and infinite. Accepting God as infinite was critical in my journey to belief and faith. A great impediment had been my inability to see how God could be very interested in me among the billions of souls in need of Divine Attention.

Then it became clear that, as God is infinite, God can divide into billions of equal and undiminished parts and give each one of us perpetual and undivided attention.

That view helped me grasp the concept of a personal God, and it still lights my path and comforts me. It helps me to consciously be a magical creature in God's Magic World.

I love you all.

June 7

Good morning.

Our keynote is "Courtesy."

Today's Meditation and Prayer discuss the growth experienced as a result of "reaching upward" for things of the spirit.

When I directly seek my own success, comfort, and happiness, they ultimately elude me, and I am left empty and embittered.

However, when I behave as a person who is not so concerned with self, seeks to be helpful to others, and stitches as the Divine Spark directs, miracles happen. The blessings which eluded me when directly sought begin to materialize. The world ceases to be a dangerous, difficult place, and I progress toward rebirth.

Thank my loving God, it is not necessary to actually achieve spiritual goals in order to be on the road to God's Magic. Persistently reaching for them is enough. The journey is the destination.

I love you all.

June 8

Good morning.

Our keynote is "Gratitude."

Today's reading urges us to choose what is good for the soul and to realize God's purpose for our lives.

Prior to sobriety, I would have understood the reading to mean that I should figure out what is good for the soul and learn God's purpose for my life. That was because I believed "to realize" meant the same as "to know."

Viewing the word "realize" as a form of the word "real" changes today's message dramatically. It becomes about doing rather than learning.

Today, "to realize" means to be brought into reality by my actions, not to be learned or understood.

If I listen for the Divine Spark and seek to take the next stitch as directed, God's purpose for my life will magically be served. By my actions, one stitch at a time, I will have persistently chosen what is good for my soul.

I form intentions with my mind, but I make decisions or choices with my feet.

I love you all.

June 9

Good morning.

Our keynote is "Humility."

Today's reading discusses faith, harmony with God, and being in the universe's stream of goodness.

Being in the stream of goodness is not accomplished by one big decision. Multiple times each day, consciously or not, I choose the direction of my life with my very next action.

At any given moment, either my brain and ego are in charge, or I am trying to do God's Will as directed by the Divine Spark.

I must persist in maintaining awareness of The Spark, or my ego will govern by default.

When I am trying to run the show, I am outside the stream of goodness. With each errant or defiant stitch, I reject faith and move further from harmony with God and my fellows.

But when I persistently seek to acknowledge, honor, and obey the Divine Spark, God is the boss. I am then in the stream of goodness and living in God's Magic.

Today, I pray to persistently accept the limits of my knowledge and power, do the next right thing, and thereby live this day in God's Magic and in harmony with my fellows.

I love you all.

June 10

Good morning.

Our keynote is "Honesty."

Today's reading discusses the process of building faith.

The faith that matters most in my life is my faithful action. Feeling faithful and being free of doubt is comfortable and makes faithful action easier, but it impacts nothing but the way I feel. It is my behavior consistent with faith which grows legs and leaves a footprint on reality.

Building faith is, for me, like an athlete exercising in order to build physical strength. The resulting increase in strength is not dependent upon the athlete wanting to do the work or even whether he or she believes it will work. If the action is persistently taken, the body will strengthen. So I have found it to be with behaving faithfully.

Regardless of my mental, emotional, or spiritual state, persistently taking the next right stitch magically restores my mind and soul while serving both God and those around me.

I love you all.

June 11

Good morning.

Our keynote is: "Humbly say to ourselves many times today, 'Thy will be done'..."

Today's Meditation and Prayer are devoted to "peace".

In my experience, reliance on my Higher Power, while seeking to do God's Will, one stitch at a time, is the only path to lasting peace. Fleeting respite may be derived from material and human things, but true, enduring peace must come from behaving in harmony with God's Will.

As my original sponsor said, there is no path to comfort other than doing things which will ultimately make me comfortable and ceasing to do things which will eventually make me uncomfortable. I must be spiritually comfortable if I am to know The Magic of God's peace.

While taking the next stitch in accord with God's Will is sometimes immediately uncomfortable, only persistence in doing so will lead me to God's Peace. No amount of prayer, AA meetings, 12th Step work, or spiritual seeking can calm my soul if I continue to put rattlesnakes under my bed.

I love you all.

June 12

Good morning.

Our keynote is: "Pray to seek to love, comfort, and understand..."

Today's reading is about recognizing, and then acting in accordance with, God's will for us. The quoted scripture promises that, if one hears and follows the directions, one stitch at a time, a solid and useful life will result.

It's actually a two-step process: recognizing the Divine Guidance and then actually doing it. Cherry, my first sponsor, warned that knowing the right thing without doing it is not useless. It is far worse than useless. If I don't recognize and acknowledge Divine Guidance for the next stitch, my life will be aimless and won't work out well.

However, if I am aware of the Divine Spark's guidance and persistently fail or refuse to comply, it will literally kill my soul. I will irretrievably smother the Divine Spark and be lost to God's Magic.

I love you all.

June 13

Good morning.

Our keynote is: "Help God's kids do what they need to have done..."

Today's Meditation promises, "...the attitude of 'Thy will, not mine, be done' leads to clear guidance".

My experience verifies that truth.

In early sobriety, a new understanding of the word "attitude" changed my life. AA members were constantly telling me that I had to change my attitude if I were to stay sober. I tried, but, believing my attitude to be the way I felt and thought, I had no immediate power to change it.

My sponsor sent me to a 1930s dictionary in which the first definition of "attitude" was a term from geometry and aviation, "angle of approach".

My angle of approach toward someone or something is the way I behave toward that person or thing, not what I am thinking or feeling. I CAN immediately change the way I behave, one stitch at a time.

Magically, my attitude went instantly from totally beyond my control to totally within my control.

That realization may have saved my life, and I have consciously used it every day since 1981.

I love you all.

June 14

Good morning.

Our keynote is "Persistence."

While the Meditation for the Day doesn't specifically mention AA's sixth and seventh steps, its theme is what I believe to be the essence of the life-changing and lifelong process of living those steps.

We are promised that if we persistently stitch as directed by the Divine Spark, we will be molded into a better likeness of God's vision for us than our self-determined ideas of how we should be.

We are told to avoid self-recrimination by never looking back and to be unfailingly courteous.

We are warned against putting off until tomorrow what we know should be done today.

Persistently seeking to follow those directions is living the sixth and seventh steps as I understand them. Doing so magically changes me and my world.

If I do my part, God will change me. I will slowly be transformed into a better, more gentle, useful, and peaceful person. God will mold me into someone far better than I ever imagined while "working on me" trying to make me into the person I thought I should be.

I love you all.

June 15

Good morning.

Today's keynote is "Courtesy."

The Meditation for the Day declares all material things to be burdens to the extent they impede our consciousness of God's Guidance.

Each day of my life is a struggle between the clamor and stress of the material world and maintaining consciousness of God and the Divine Spark.

If I turn all my interest, attention, and love to the material world, I find no true satisfaction and may become blind and deaf to God's Guidance.

I am then a menace to myself and others.

However, if I turn that interest, attention, and love to God and the needs of my fellows, the material world falls into place. I then find satisfaction and joy in both the material and spiritual and am once again aware of being a magical creature in God's Magic World.

I am home.

I love you all.

June 16

Good morning.

Our keynote is "Gratitude."

Today's Meditation directs us to seek God early in the day before God consciousness is lost in life's problems, tasks, or pleasures.

AA's Big Book urges us to, ON AWAKENING, ask God to direct our thinking, especially asking that it be divorced from self-pity, dishonest or self-seeking motives.

My sponsor explained that if the book meant us to offer that prayer after visiting the bathroom, it would have said so.

His directions were to do it immediately on awakening for two reasons.

First, I desperately need to follow directions to the letter, and second, I am crazy enough to ruin the day, or even the rest of my life, between the bed and the bathroom.

Years of persistence in running that prayer through my head within seconds of becoming conscious has worked magic.

It causes me to think of God before I engage the world, making it less likely that I will squander the day lost in self-centered chaos.

I love you all.

June 17

Good morning.

Our keynote is "Humility."

Today's Meditation is about maintaining consciousness of God throughout the day. I call it "The other 95% of the 11th Step". It is 11th Step action taken continuously between my morning and evening prayer and meditation routines.

Persistent awareness of God is so important that I often think it is the panacea. Nothing has been more effective in keeping me aware of the Divine than the simple instructions from the Big Book.

If I pause when agitated or doubtful, constantly remind myself I am no longer running the show and humbly say to myself many times each day, "Thy will be done," magic happens. The immensely practical 11th Step promises materialize. I am in much less danger of excitement, fear, anger, worry, self-pity, or foolish decisions. I am more efficient and energetic.

Simple and practical, it works. It really does.

I love you all.

June 18

Good morning.

Our keynote is "Honesty."

Today's Meditation is clear that no amount of prayer and quiet communion with God can, by itself, constitute a full spiritual life. Of course, those things are absolutely necessary, but it isn't until we are, in some manner, sharing our spiritual experience with others that we are indeed living a spiritual life.

We don't need a podium or people coming to us for guidance in order to share our spirituality. We share it when we show love, courtesy, consideration, or interest to another human being. To be able to brighten the day of an intimate or a stranger with a smile, courtesy, or a kind word is a magical power! The more joy and peace we seek to transmit to others, the more joy and peace we know. In my experience, that is God's way.

Not only must I give it away to keep it, I must give it away in order to ever receive it in full measure. "The spiritual life is not a theory. We have to live it." (BB, p.83.)

I love you all.

June 19

Good morning.

Our keynote is "Humbly say to ourselves many times today, 'Thy will be done'..."

Today's reading declares work on the material plane to be secondary to our primary objective of seeking spiritual growth. AA's Big Book affirms the principle in stating, "Material well-being always follows spiritual growth; it is never the other way around."

Yet, we all know, or know of, materially wealthy people who do not appear to be concerned with spirituality. I don't believe the principle of "spirituality first" is contradicted by the financially well off who don't have a spiritual basis.

Having an abundance of earthly things and enjoying material well-being are not the same thing. Often people with the most money are in the greatest fear of financial insecurity. And, many who are of extremely modest means live in comfortable assurance of God's bounty.

I find The Magic in seeking to follow the Divine Spark's direction and serve others, while being content and secure with that which God provides materially. In stumbling so imperfectly, but persistently, along that path for four decades, God has never let me down.

I love you all.

June 20

Good morning.

Our keynote is "Pray to seek to love, comfort, and understand…"

Today's Meditation tells us that we realize God's Power in the material world by viewing God through the eyes of faith. Thoughts and feelings of faith make it easier to do the right thing as well as bringing feelings of security and well-being. But sometimes my intellectual faith weakens, and I can't immediately bring it back in full force.

Happily, I have found my access to The Divine to remain available despite periods of waning intellectual faith. The Power is triggered in my material world not so much by my state of mind as by my demonstration of faith. A demonstration of faith is behaving in accordance with faith and, magically, works independently of the crazy picture show in my head. Only my actions (never my thoughts, feelings, or beliefs) ever leave a footprint on reality.

Faithful behavior grants me access to God's Grace and Power regardless of my uncertain mind and emotions. Persistently taking faithful action IS viewing God through the eyes of faith.

I love you all.

June 21

Good morning.

Our keynote is "Help God's kids do what they need to have done..."

The 24 Hour Book reading for today declares a serene and sane mind to be unattainable through reasoning, learning, or trying to directly adjust our own spiritual state. I can't learn or pray enough to find peace if my behavior is insane and/or frantic.

In order to attain and maintain sanity and serenity, the first two things I must do are:

1. Persist in seeking to do the right thing one stitch at a time. I am guaranteed stress and chaos if I persistently behave contrary to God's Will for me.
2. Avoid "big deals" like the plague. Big deals excite me, inflate my ego, and destroy my effectiveness. They are mutually exclusive with serenity. My ego will make a big deal of anything it can somehow connect with itself. In reality, when I make a big deal of anything other than God or the 12 Steps, I am making myself the big deal.

I find The Magic of sanity and serenity only if I seek to behave in accordance with God's Will and have NO BIG DEALS.

I love you all.

June 22

Good morning.

Our keynote is "Persistence".

Today's reading warns against thinking of the sea of difficulties which lies ahead.

I have squandered far too much time and energy vainly petitioning God on Tuesday to give me the strength to handle Wednesday. I am never given what I need to cope with tomorrow until it becomes today.

My dear friend, Leon, states that when he chooses to go into the future God says, "Have a good time, Leon, I will be here when you get back."

If I go into the future, I go alone and unprotected. The only place and time God can be found is here and now.

Addressing the human tendency to live in the "wreckage of the future," Mark Twain said, "My life has been filled with many tragedies; almost none of which ever happened."

I pray to truly live in The Magic of this day, behaving as if I know I am secure in God's hands and will remain so when (or if) tomorrow becomes today.

I love you all.

June 23

Good morning.

Our keynote is "Courtesy".

Today's Meditation and Prayer urge resting to become recharged and pausing to await the renewal of our strength.

Of course, I can't outrun God, but I do outrun my God consciousness. It usually happens when I allow myself to have "big deals" that convince me that my little plans and designs are too important and urgent for me to take time to think of God. I am then frantically rushing down a perilous path with no compass but my own fevered brain and ego.

God has salvaged many of those days when I have paused and started the day over. I can start a brand-new 24 hours anytime and any place. I have subtly done it on my knees by my desk, in men's rooms, etc. When getting on my knees would have been inappropriate or impossible, I have done it while driving, cross-examining witnesses, and in countless other situations.

It works by returning me to calmness, clear-headed effectiveness, and The Magic of being guided by the Divine Spark.

I love you all.

June 24

Good morning.

Our keynote is "Gratitude".

Today's reading warns against allowing personal piques and resentments to drive our behavior.

A few harsh words or a single thoughtless act can damage or destroy a relationship built by years of courtesy and consideration. As my dear friend from early sobriety, Jimmy P., says, "It takes very little horse manure to ruin a world of ice cream."

I don't have an "off button" to prevent feeling piqued or resentful. However, I am provided with tools to keep such feelings from lingering and prevent me from acting on them and, thereby, allowing them to impact reality.

Maintaining conscious contact with God and being persistently courteous are my first line of defense against lashing out hurtfully or otherwise being offensive. Even when negative emotions roil, repetitive silent prayer to seek to love, comfort, and understand rather than to be loved, comforted, and understood brings the right words, actions, and demeanor to nurture my relationships rather than lay waste to them.

That prayer consistently has a magical effect on my human relations.

I love you all.

June 25

Good morning.

Our keynote is "Humility".

Today's Meditation discusses the value of contemplating God's great creation in sacred awe.

I have squandered many days taking God's Magic, of which we are each a tiny, magical part, for granted.

Two great gifts flow from contemplating God's universe in awe. First, it fosters humility to realize my smallness relative to God's vast creation. Second, awareness of the priceless miracle and blessing of being alive, conscious, and sober today fills me with gratitude.

In the resulting light of humility and gratitude, I am aware that this day of human life is a greater blessing and victory than winning Powerball. My difficulties fade to nothingness.

I am then freed from myself to seek to be useful and kind to all the other little magical parts of God who walk this earth.

I love you all.

June 26

Good morning.

Our keynote is "Honesty".

Today's Meditation and Prayer caution us against acting rashly without seeking Divine Guidance.

My tendency to act rashly is fueled by "big deals". My ego tells me that something (always boiling down to MYSELF) is so important that I must react immediately.

God built instantaneous guidance into our instincts to handle real emergencies such as jumping out of the path of a speeding vehicle.

It is in routine situations that I blow my own importance out of all proportion, which causes me to think I'm under too much pressure to wait for God's guidance. That is when I make my worst messes because my big deals have robbed me of God consciousness.

When I can think of nothing but the "big deal", I am alone and lost in my own chaos.
The Big Book directs us to pause when agitated or doubtful and ask for the right thought or action.

I find The Magic by following those directions; never through my frantic self-centered reactions.

I love you all.

June 27

Good morning.

Our keynote is: "Humbly say to ourselves many times today 'Thy will be done',...".

Today's Meditation and Prayer emphasize passing our blessings on to others.

We never know the full impact of seeking to be helpful or even giving a person a smile and just a moment of our interest, attention and love.

One of the greatest examples of a single blessing going around the world is AA itself. The salvation and enrichment of millions of lives all started with Bill Wilson sharing his blessing of sobriety by giving his entire interest, attention and love to Dr. Bob on Mother's Day of 1935.

When I seek to share my own blessings, they grow, but when I try to keep them for myself they usually evaporate. The origin and engine of my alcoholism is self centeredness. I cannot effectively treat it by any form of self obsession, even if I dress my preoccupation with me in spiritual clothing.

Seeking to share my blessings magically brings the greatest of all blessings to me, freedom from the bondage of self.

I love you all.

June 28

Good morning.

Our keynote is: "Pray to seek to love, comfort and understand, ...".

Today's reading advocates adjusting one's attitude to focus on doing God's will in the present while leaving the future to God. As long as I believed my attitude to be my state of mind and how I felt, it was impossible to immediately adjust.

The definition of "attitude" that changed my life is, "angle of approach".

My angle of approach is not what I think, feel or believe. It is how I behave toward something or someone.

When I define my attitude as my behavior, rather than my thoughts, feelings and beliefs, I am magically in immediate control of my attitude, one stitch at a time.

Regardless of my doubts, fears and reluctance, when I behave as a person who is confident that God has the future in hand, that is my attitude. When so behaving, I eventually get all the benefits of having such an attitude, including being free to do the best I can in the right now.

I love you all.

June 29

Good morning.

Today's keynote is: "Help God's kids do what they need to have done..."

The Meditation and Prayer for the Day emphasize God's preparation of us for better things to come.

In my experience, that preparation includes times when I can't see how anything positive could possibly come from my immediate difficulties, mistakes, and failures. I am never able to see God's long-term objectives, and often the preparation for them involves failure, doubt, fear, and feeling hopeless.

My key to getting past the failures and hopelessness has proved to be persistence. Perhaps my deadliest enemy is the inner voice that tells me I have failed so miserably that there is no hope... no longer a next right thing to do. It is the Big Lie.

Every significant personal or professional success in my life has, at some point, felt like it was going to be a colossal disaster. God's delays in helping with painful and embarrassing character defects turned out to be an essential part of the message I carry today.

The times when I can't see or feel any magic at all are, themselves, part of The Magic.

I love you all.

June 30

Good morning.

Our keynote is "Persistence".

Today's reading is about the necessity of living in the NOW.

I have wasted much of my life fearfully probing the future or wallowing in guilt and remorse over the past.

The problem with going into the future or the past is threefold:

1. Neither God nor human fellowship can be found in either. Outside of the present, I am totally alone.
2. Without God, I have no guidance. The Divine Spark speaks only in the right now. So, in the past or future, I am befuddled.
3. The only power I ever have is over my own next action. I cannot take action in either the past or the future, so I am powerless outside of this instant.

When I am alone, befuddled, and powerless, there is no magic.

The Magic is only in the NOW.

I love you all.

JULY

July 1

Good morning.

Our keynote is "Courtesy".

Today's Meditation and Prayer urge us to remain calm and try to pass that calmness to others.

Having big deals is the primary destroyer of my calmness and peace. In the grip of my "big dealism", I am crippled by ego, fear, doubt, and worry, and I similarly poison those around me. I will not embrace the pervasive myth that worry is somehow useful or noble. Worry and fear don't heighten my abilities. They rob me of them.

Big deals further assault calmness by fueling my demands to be loved, comforted, and understood.

The soul storms I create with my self-importance subside only when I strive to maintain God consciousness, behave like a person who doesn't have big deals, and seek to love, comfort, and understand others.

When I do those things, my fear, worry, and doubt are chased away by God's Magic.

Only then do I have calmness, peace, and faith to pass to others.

I love you all.

July 2

Good morning.

Our keynote is "Gratitude".

Today's reading refers to the biblical declaration that we must come as little children if we are to enter the kingdom of heaven. In my "evangelical agnosticism", I thought that was the greatest nonsense in a book filled with nonsense.

For decades now, I have believed it to be profoundly valid and the very basis of faith, spirituality, success, and usefulness.

A little child often has no understanding of what the parent is doing or where he or she is being taken. Yet, the child of a loving parent is comfortable and secure in faith that the parent loves them and knows what is best.

Like a little child, I don't understand God's Magic World, where I'm being taken, or God's purpose.

In order to travel the road to God's Magic, I must behave like a comfortable and secure child who trusts The Parent. I do so by obeying the Divine Spark, one stitch at a time, especially when my "adult" brain and ego clearly have a better idea!

I love you all.

July 3

Good morning.

Our keynote is "Humility".

Today's reading discusses life's spiritually unexplored country and the wonderful discoveries awaiting those who seek to walk the spiritual path. It emphasizes our inability to predict or understand the patterns of our lives.

The future is never seen until it becomes the present. It is unknown territory for which there are no maps or GPS apps.

I am reminded that my primary problem with perfection is not my inability to attain it.

I hit the wall way before that point. My problem is my inability to recognize perfection, which means I don't know who or what God wants me to be.

The full extent of my certain knowledge of God's will and my real power are both limited to the single next thing God wants me to do or say.

When I accept those limitations and persistently try to take the next stitch as directed, God's Magic takes over. A future unfolds which is different from, and far better than, anything I could have imagined.

God lights my path with a penlight for a single step; never with a floodlight.

I love you all.

July 4

Good morning.

Our keynote is: "Honesty".

Today's Meditation and Prayer urge viewing God as a friend.

Perceiving God as either an ultra busy CEO or the vengeful God of the Old Testament did not promote a feeling that God and I could be pals. And, considering the billions of people, how could God possibly be a constantly present friend to each of us?

In early sobriety I began to realize that, if God is infinite, God can divide into an unlimited number of equal, all powerful parts and devote full time to each one of us. Realizing what God's infinity really means opened the door to anytime contact and friendship with God. Talking with God as I would an earthly friend helps me feel the magic of God's friendship.

The more I cultivate my friendship with God, the better friend I am to my fellows. And, magically, the better friend I am to my fellows, the better and more profound is my friendship with God.

I love you all.

July 5

Good morning.

Our keynote is: "Humbly say to ourselves many times today, 'Thy will be done, ...".

Today's reading discusses God's readiness to come to our aid when we surrender trying to do it on our own. When I finally surrender God's response often comes quickly.

Fueled by various forms of self will, I paint myself into corners. When I first pick up the paint brush it isn't labeled "self will". I may see it as responsibility, security, common sense or even a self determined spiritual pursuit. I set out painting with more awareness of my "big deal" than of the Divine Spark. Eventually, I realize I am hopelessly painted into the corner.

It is proof of God's mercy that I don't have to undo all my ill advised activity in order to get out of the corner and back into harmony with God and my fellows.
I simply have to lay down the paintbrush and say, " Oops!

I'm sorry. I did it again. Please show me the next right stitch". As soon as I resume stitching as directed, I am, magically, out of the corner and back on track. My burdens slip away and my mountains become mole hills.

God's love, forgiveness and mercy are always just a surrender away.

I love you all.

July 6

Good morning.

Our keynote is: "Pray to seek to love, comfort, and understand..."

Today's Meditation and Prayer discuss accessing God's strength and power. Our reading explains that we access the Almighty by our faith.

I agree, but effective "faith" means something different to me than it meant in the past. I used to believe "faith" meant believing and feeling that I am safely nestled in God's hands. I am now convinced that real faith is action; specifically, seeking to do God's will, one stitch at a time.

That realization has been, and continues to be, life-changing.

Magically, if my behavior is consistent with faith, God's strength and power flow in, regardless of my faltering intellectual faith.

However, I can be convinced I have faith but, if my actions are not faithful, God's strength and power are denied me.

I access God with my feet, not my brain.

That is good news because, while I can never immediately control my mind, I can always control my next action.

I love you all.

July 7

Good morning.

Our keynote is "Help God's kids do what they need to have done".

Today's reading tells us that selfishness and pride often make us want things that are not good for us. In retrospect, I can clearly see times when God protected others and me by prayers seemingly unanswered or answered in a form that I didn't want or anticipate. Without divine guidance, I simply don't know what's good for me. Therefore, my only hope always has been, and remains, to come as a little child and follow God's guidance, regardless of what I think, feel, or believe.

In this regard, God often sets me aright through the magic of spiritual fellowship. My insane ideas tend to introduce themselves as common sense, and my flawed perception is inclined to believe them. The magic of fellowship is that my insane ideas never sound like common sense to you, and your insane ideas never sound like common sense to me.

I love you all.

July 8

Good morning.

Our keynote is "Persistence".

Today's reading urges cooperation with God's force for good in the world. When I first began awakening to the truth that we are spiritual creatures in God's Magic World, I had a mistaken idea of how one becomes a part of the force for good. I believed it to be a matter of getting my thoughts, feelings, and beliefs in order, and then I would automatically be part of the force for good. I would consistently want to do the next right thing.

My experience has been very different. Forming an intention to be part of God's force for good is merely the starting point. My intention is transformed into the reality of a decision only by persistently renewing it with every single stitch. While I make many errant stitches, if I keep stumbling in the right direction I move closer to the force for good with each failure followed by renewed right action. I am not capable of perfection, and God seems to be quite pleased with the best I can do, which is persistence.

I love you all.

July 9

Good morning.

Our keynote is "Courtesy".

Today's reading encourages us to continue on our venture of faith, despite intellectual doubt. One of my daily prayers is, "Lord, I believe. Please help my unbelief." Episodes of intellectual doubt can do no real harm unless I allow them to impact my behavior.

It is my action consistent with faith that gets results, not the degree of my intellectual certainty of God's love and protection. Persistent faithful behavior while plagued by doubts is the most valuable spiritual action I can take. The magic of such action is twofold: first, I get all the benefits of faith; second, I am returned to the belief and feeling that I am safe in God's hands. By acts of faith, doubts are chased away, leaving no footprint on reality. It is a great gift that God's magic is found through my behavior, which I can immediately control, not my mind, over which I have no immediate control.

I love you all.

July 10

Good morning.

Our keynote is "Gratitude."

Today's reading is largely devoted to the miraculous changes in people who persistently seek God. Those of us in AA see these miracles so often that we are in danger of taking them for granted. I pray to maintain sacred awe at the power of God to change a hopeless drunk into a force for good.

In working with others, I must always keep in mind that I cannot bring about the miracle. As the 12th Step indicates, I can only carry the message, not deliver it. Delivery is up to God and the other person. If I make a big deal of my role as a messenger, I can't help very many people. The burden of assuming responsibility for the sobriety of others is too great. However, if I accept the limitation of my power to simply speak and live the quiet, loving truth, I am magically positioned to be used by God as a humble tool or channel. I most effectively carry the message when I concentrate on what I can do and don't waste time and energy on that which can only be accomplished by God.

I love you all.

July 11

Good morning.

Our keynote is "Humility."

The Thought for the Day affirms a force for good in the universe and suggests we ask ourselves if we are in this stream of goodness. I am convinced that I can't think, learn, talk, or even pray my way into the stream of goodness. It is my belief that with every loving, considerate, helpful, or comforting act toward my fellows, I honor God's will and step into the stream of goodness.

On the other hand, I believe just as strongly that when selfishness prevails and I am unkind, inconsiderate, discourteous, or unhelpful to those around me, I fall out of step with goodness and God's will. Magically, each right stitch I make feeds the stream of goodness in the universe, but just as surely, each errant stitch drains it. Whether or not I am in the stream of goodness is determined by my actions towards humankind, not by well-meaning or even spiritual obsession on myself. Today, I pray to heed the Divine Spark with each stitch, treating my fellows with love and courtesy. Only to the extent I succeed in heeding The Spark will I be part of the force for good.

I love you all.

July 12

Good morning.

Our keynote is "Honesty."

Today's reading emphasizes that it is not God's nature to lift us out of our personal hells only to abandon us to our own devices. Realizing the extent of God's love and forgiveness has come to me slowly and still evaporates at times. In early sobriety, I began to glimpse the reality of God's grace and forgiveness. However, I strongly suspected that I had exhausted it. I felt like a criminal defendant granted totally undeserved and unexpected probation but told by the judge, "If you mess up again, there will be no more mercy."

Gratefully, it turns out that it was I, not God, imposing an unrealistic demand for perfection. The magic is that God's love and forgiveness are inexhaustible, and I need them every day in the smallest and largest of matters. God only rarely shields me from the natural consequences of my behavior but will never withhold forgiveness and love.

I love you all.

July 13

Good morning.

Our keynote is "Humbly say to ourselves many times today, 'Thy will be done'..."

Today's reading urges us to expect God to bring better things.

Multiple times each day, I get to choose my "pair of glasses."

On one hand, I can choose to live in fear of the future and project into all the worst things that can happen. Wearing those glasses, I frequently cause the worst to happen by my frantic, self-centered flailing about.

Or, I can choose childlike expectant curiosity and joyful anticipation about how God will weave my "mess of the moment" into something beautiful.

Often, I must assist God in changing my view of the future by praying and then behaving like one who expects to be showered with God's love, forgiveness, and bounty as the future unfolds. When I choose that angle of approach, the magic happens; God replaces my impotent self-centered terror with childlike faith, expectant curiosity, and joyful anticipation.

I have a new pair of glasses!

I love you all.

July 14

Good morning.

Our keynote is "Pray to seek to love, comfort, and understand..."

The Prayer for the Day asks that I may go forward unafraid and be under God's protection as long as I serve God. The wording presumes that the prayer will be in vain if I fail to seek to do God's will.

I cannot expect God's protection if I pray for God's will for me but proceed to go about doing my own will.

Also, "going forward unafraid" doesn't mean that all fear must be driven from my mind and heart before I can get about the business of doing God's will. Instead, it means behaving as if I were unafraid by taking the next stitch as directed by the Divine Spark, even though I remain fearful.

God does not remove my fear just because I ask for its removal. It is usually removed only after I begin positive action following prayer.

Magically, if, despite my fear, my prayer is followed by right action, I come under God's protection and begin to feel unafraid.

I love you all.

July 15

Good morning.

Our keynote is "Help God's kids do what they need to have done..."

Today's reading uses "climbing up the ladder of life" as an analogy for seeking to live a spiritual life.

I believe it is the same journey which I describe as "stitching as the Divine Spark directs."

We are urged to "climb the ladder" without fear or doubt.

While trying to take the next step up the ladder, I find persistent consciousness of God to be essential.

I have successfully used many simple reminders to think of God more often, but I have found nothing more useful than the Big Book's discussion of the 11th step. Therein it is suggested that we humbly say to ourselves many times each day, "Thy will be done."

Following that simple direction makes my climb much easier.

It chases away fear and doubt by persistently affirming my awareness of God.

I am then far more likely to be in tune with God's Magic.

I love you all.

July 16

Good morning.

Our keynote is "Persistence".

The Thought for the Day suggests wearing the world like a loose garment. I believe that biblical reference can be paraphrased as "No Big Deals!"

Anytime I make a big deal of anything (whether I view it as good or bad) other than God or the 12 steps, I am actually making a big deal of myself.

In the throes of my "big deals," I am driven by ego and crippled by stress. Peace and serenity cannot coexist with big deals.

None of the highly successful people I have known ever seemed to have big deals. However, every chronic failure of my acquaintance has been consumed by them. They are weakened and rendered ineffective by the weight of their big deals. The weakness and ineffectiveness manifest itself in both the material and spiritual realms.

I pray today to live in God's Magic by having only little deals.

I love you all.

July 17

Good morning.

Our keynote is "Courtesy".

Today's reading cautions that God's power and guidance are blocked by selfishness, intellectual pride, fear, greed, and materialism.

While I agree, the biggest factor limiting my access to The Divine is my failure to simply maintain God consciousness.

In early sobriety, I would spend a few minutes each morning and evening in thoughts of God and call myself having done the 11th step. I would rarely think of God during the other 95% of the day. At best, I had done only 5% of the 11th step.

By not actively seeking to maintain God consciousness, I open the door to all the things that block me from God's power and guidance.

Morning and evening prayer and meditation are absolutely essential. However, I find even greater magic by using reminders of God throughout the other 95% of the day.

Anything that will remind me of God, from a rubber band on my wrist to holding the door to a room or car, will enhance my consciousness of God.

Awareness of God is the closest thing I have found to the panacea. It charms my human interactions and shields me from fear, worry, doubt, frustration, and foolish decisions.

I love you all.

July 18

Good morning.

Our keynote is "Gratitude".

Today's Meditation and Prayer tell us that being grateful to God, while walking humbly, will impress others and make us more effective messengers.

I love the wording, "walking humbly".

If I try to figure out how to become humble, I get nowhere. There is nothing intellectual or psychological about humility. The instant my mind thinks I have gained some humility, by definition, I have not.

There are blessed messengers among us who, by their actions and demeanor, exude humility and gratitude.

The best I can do is pray to BE like those blessed messengers and then proceed to BEHAVE like them.

I believe I am effective as a messenger only to the extent that I persistently walk in the footprints of those who show me the way.

Magically, when I persist in emulating the behavior of giants, I may be blessed with a little bit of their effectiveness.

I love you all.

July 19

Good morning.

Our keynote is "Humility."

Today's Meditation and Prayer emphasize the necessity of doing our footwork if God's miracles are to be brought into reality.

Apparently, God enjoys partnering with us.

The seed from which AA grew was Bill W.'s spiritual experience while withdrawing from alcohol in a hospital bed in 1934.

However, if Bill had written off his experience as DT's, or otherwise failed to follow up, AA would not exist.

Neither Bill nor Dr. Silkworth knew what had happened. The next morning, the doctor said, "I don't know what it was either, Bill, but if I were you, I would hold on to it. It's got to be better than what you had." The moment Bill began acting on the doctor's advice is the true beginning of AA.

Bill merely forming an intention to treat it as a spiritual experience would have accomplished nothing.

Acting on God's intervention transformed Bill's intention into a decision, which caused a "smoking bush" to become a burning bush.

The partnership between the nudge from God and Bill's lifelong action in response triggered God's power and grace and magically brought about the miracle of AA.

I pray to work in partnership with God today.

I love you all.

July 20

Good morning.

Our keynote is "Honesty."

Today's reading directs us to follow God's guidance the best we can and leave the results to God.

In my experience, that simple idea is the key to a useful, peaceful, joyous, and successful life.

It's no longer difficult for me to intellectually know that the only glimpse of God's will I ever get is in the absolute right now and the only power I ever have is over my very next action.

My perennial problem is with translating knowledge of those limitations into action. Facing the extent of my mind's impotence is so offensive to my ego that it can paralyze me. It's just too simple.

Accepting that my little brain is truly so limited feels like a death of self, but persistence in doing so opens the door for God's grace and power.

Magically, when I say a prayer and then proceed to behave as a person would behave if they accepted their limitations, everything falls into place.

Bill W. called that simple idea the "keystone of the arch through which we walk to freedom."

So do I.

I love you all.

July 21

Good morning.

Our keynote is: "Humbly say to ourselves many times today, 'Thy will be done'..."

The Thought for the Day asks if I am truly tolerant.

It reminds me of the AA Code which is, "love and tolerance of others."

I used to believe the ability to ignore irritating behavior or distressing situations was tolerance, but now realize tolerance requires more of me.

Tolerance is much like forgiveness. If I am to be comfortably sober, I sometimes must forgive and tolerate things that feel unforgivable or intolerable.

Gratefully, the AA Code does not require me to feel loving and tolerant in order to behave that way.

Today, I judge my level of tolerance by my behavior, not by my thoughts and feelings.

Magically, God moves mountains in my personal relationships when my behavior is loving and tolerant.

Also, by behaving in accordance with the AA Code, I begin to have a loving and tolerant mind.

I can never heal my mind with my mind. My mind is healed (if at all) with my feet.

I love you all.

July 22

Good morning.

Our keynote is: "Pray to seek to love, comfort and understand..."

Today's Meditation continues to emphasize the power we are given to do good works through our partnership with God.

The Prayer for the Day asks that I not limit myself by allowing my doubting mind to stop me from trying to carry the message.

Many times I have stood at a podium or participated in a conversation feeling I had nothing to give. I have felt unworthy, disconnected from God and my fellows, and obsessed with my own problems.

By doing the best I could to be helpful, despite my doubt, I have repeatedly been told that God helped someone through my words and actions when I felt spiritually bankrupt.

Magically, if I continue to stitch as the Divine Spark guides, God's power and grace flow unimpeded by my assessment of my spiritual condition.

I love you all.

July 23

Good morning.

Our keynote is: "Help God's kids do what they need to have done..."

Today's Meditation and Prayer address the importance of maintaining inner peace and calm.

My most effective approach to that end is threefold:

1. Maintaining God consciousness throughout the day connects me with the only true source of peace and calm.
2. Avoiding "big deals," good or bad, keeps turmoil and distractions at bay.
3. Persistently praying to give my entire interest, attention and love to others while seeking to love, comfort, and understand them keeps my mind off myself. My most frequent source of "soul storms" is concern with being loved, comforted, and understood to my satisfaction.

Persistent use of the above tools loosens the bondage of self and allows me to sometimes touch The Magic of God's perfect peace and calm.

I love you all.

July 24

Good morning.

Our keynote is "Persistence."

Today's reading promises that seeking to behave and live as though we are always in the presence of God is the solution to most of the world's problems and the secret of personal power.

It confirms my own experience that conscious awareness of God is the closest thing to the panacea. It is the cure for all ills and the answer to every question.

I don't believe I have ever gotten in trouble for anything I did or said while I was thinking of God.

A few of the ways I can "practice the presence of God" are:

1. Humbly saying to myself many times each day, "Thy will be done."
2. Holding the door of a room or car just a heartbeat for God to go in before me.
3. Using a rubber band around my wrist or a strategically placed note to remind me of God.
4. Carrying on a running conversation with God.

Such simple actions help connect me with God's Magic, which is all the power of the universe.

I love you all.

July 25

Good morning.

Our keynote is "Courtesy."

Today's reading urges us to hold our lives in trust for God and no longer consider them our own. How is it possible for a human being's angle of approach to be so drastically changed from my natural obsession with, and reliance upon, self? The only answer I have found is God's grace and power coupled with my seeking to do God's will one stitch at a time.

I will never be able to pray, educate, or even behave myself into constant and permanent awareness that my life belongs to God. In the midst of my human affairs, my consciousness of that fact slips away multiple times every day. However, if I persistently remind myself of God's supremacy and ask for forgiveness and fresh guidance after each errant, selfish stitch, magic happens.

My life gradually begins to bear a slight resemblance to a life that has been placed in trust for God. I find God's Magic by persistent (and often corrective) right action, not through my mind or the myth of human perfection.

I love you all.

July 26

Good morning.

Our keynote is "Gratitude."

The Thought for the Day declares that, at the end of our lives, material acquisitions will amount to nothing. The only things we will take out of this world are what we have done for others.

I agree, but my experience is that the rewards for serving others begin long before the end of this life. For 37 years, I tried to live for me and wound up losing everything and everyone, including myself. For the most recent decades of my life, I have been aware that the proper angle of approach is seeking to help God's kids do what they need to have done and leaving my own care in God's hands.

My execution on that lofty goal is so inconsistent that I sometimes have to start over 50 to 100 times a day. It has often felt that my selfishness is so profound that I am hopeless. However, despite my stumbling and frustration with the slowness of progress, I have persisted. As a result of that persistence, my life today is infinitely richer and more satisfying than when I was living for myself. It is a Divine Paradox. It is enlightened self-interest. It is Magic!

I love you all.

July 27

Our keynote is "Humility."

Today's Meditation and Prayer urge "walking humbly with God" while practicing the presence of God in our daily affairs.

For me, the "practice" is behaving as though God is standing beside me throughout the day. I consistently do morning and evening prayer and meditation. Where I often fall short is during the rest of the day. My morning and evening spiritual routines take less than 5% of my waking hours and, therefore, are less than 5% of the 11th step.

The Magic is in practicing continuous awareness of God, not just checking in a couple of times a day. I have experienced life-changing results from persistently following the Big Book's all-day 11th step instructions.

It suggests I do three things:

1. Pause when agitated or doubtful and ask for the right thought or action.
2. Constantly remind myself that I am no longer running the show.
3. Humbly say to myself many times each day, "Thy will be done."

My life is far better when I follow those directions.

I love you all.

July 28

Our keynote is "Honesty."

Today's reading returns to the theme of inward peace. In my experience, seeking to remain aware of God, praying, being courteous, and avoiding "big deals" are all necessary for peace to be possible. However, I can do all those things and peace will still elude me unless I do things that ultimately make me peaceful and refrain from doing things that cause guilt, worry, or fear. If, by my actions or my failure to act (i.e., procrastination), I figuratively put rattlesnakes under my bed, I cannot expect to sleep peacefully. I deny myself The Magic of God's peace if my behavior is contrary to God's will.

I love you all.

July 29

Good morning.

Our keynote is "Humbly say to ourselves many times today, 'Thy will be done'..."

The Thought for the Day warns against morbid reflection on the past. My original sponsor, Cherry, repeatedly declared self-recrimination to be the single most useless and counterproductive of all human endeavors. My friend, Leon, shares that if he goes into the past or the future, God says, "Have a good time, Leon. I will be here when you get back."

The AA Big Book makes it clear that dwelling on our mistakes and failures will diminish our ability to help others. Right now is the only place I can find God. If I go into the past, I go alone and without God's protection. Many times I have used Emmet Fox's wonderful Golden Key to redirect my thoughts from the abyss of the past to God. It restores me to God's Magic.

I love you all.

July 30

Good morning.

Our keynote is "Pray to seek to love, comfort, and understand..."

The Thought for the Day underscores the futility of trying to live in tomorrow. When projecting into the future, I am without God as surely as when I am crawling around in the past. My tendency to seek out and focus on the worst possible outcome ensures that excursions into the future will result in anxiety and fear, unsoftened by the loving God I left behind in the present.

The actuality is that the worst very rarely happens. So, I anguish over tragedies that never become reality. Another pitfall in projection is that I will never correctly foresee tomorrow. I have wasted much of my life trying to figure out the patterns so I will know where and how to take the next stitch. Yet, I have never figured out a single pattern correctly.

I am guided by the Divine Spark only in the right now. The future is never revealed to me. I find The Magic by coming as a little child and giving my entire interest, attention, and love to the right now.

I love you all.

July 31

Good morning.

Our keynote is: "Help God's kids do what they need to have done..."

The previous two readings warned that we are on our own and without God if we go into the past or the future. It is a challenge to persistently accept the limitation of my power to my own very next action. Likewise, my ego doesn't readily agree that my knowledge of God's will goes no further than the Divine Spark's guidance for my next action.

However, persisting in that angle of approach has assured me that God has given me power and knowledge enough. The Magic is that God's power and grace flow in when I accept the limits of my own knowledge and power. I am then free to live in the right now and focus on what I CAN do and understand. My time and energy are no longer squandered by flailing blindly and impotently at things beyond my power and understanding.

I love you all.

AUGUST

August 1

Good morning.

Our keynote is "Persistence".

The Prayer for the Day asks that we may be in harmony with "...the music of the spheres".

It brings to mind a life-changing angle of approach which I began to persistently employ many years ago.

Each day when I awaken, the universe is playing a program of music divinely formulated for that day. It may not suit me or even resemble my idea of the perfect tune for the day.

However, in my experience, the universe never takes requests; I am never able to change a note of the day's concert.

My choices today, and every day, are limited to the following:

1. Descend into chaos and impotence by railing against the day's "music" and vainly trying to change the program.
2. Sulk in the corner and refuse to acknowledge, much less dance to, the music.

Or...

3. Accept that I cannot change the tune, behave as if I trust The Composer, look for the beauty in today's program, and persist in trying to dance to this day's music.

I can only be in tune with God's Magic by embracing the third choice.

I love you all.

August 2

Good morning.

Our keynote is "Courtesy".

Today's Meditation and Prayer revisit the partnership between God's grace and power and our footwork.

My loving God will do almost anything for me, but will often do almost nothing without my cooperation. For instance, I can ask God to take away a toothache, and God will do so, but only after I add the action of going to a dentist.

I turn things over to God with my feet, not my mind.

Farmers don't grow things. They create an environment in which growth will take place, and God grows things. Likewise, a physician does not heal, but creates a situation in which healing will take place and God heals.

On my own, I am incapable of changing myself, or even comprehending what changes need to be made.

However, if I will come as a little child and take each single stitch as directed by the Divine Spark, God will magically stitch as directed by the Divine Spark, God will magically move me toward what I should be.

I love you all.

August 3

Good morning.

Our keynote is "Gratitude".

Today's Meditation and Prayer discuss "serving God".

Worshipping, praying to, and communing with God are beautiful and necessary endeavors. However, they are not actually serving God; they are preparing us to serve God.

The only way I have found to actually serve God is to love, comfort, and understand God's other kids.

There is scripture to the effect that whatever we do to, or for, the least among us, we are doing to, or for, God.

When I give of my time and resources to another's benefit, I am serving God.

When I am discourteous, cruel, or dismissive to one of God's children, I am discourteous, cruel, or dismissive to God.

All of God's kids are magical creatures and are part of God.

I pray to treat them as such today.

I love you all.

August 4

Good morning.

Our keynote is "Humility".

The Thought for the Day discusses being effective in carrying the message of recovery.

In my experience, the best approach to 12th-step work is also the most effective way to carry any spiritual message.

If I am to be helpful, I first must maintain a demeanor which encourages others to approach me. We get few opportunities to be helpful if people don't feel comfortable talking with us.

Next, I need to truly listen by giving the person in front of me my entire interest, attention, and love. When I employ that angle of approach, people are more receptive to the quiet, loving truth of my own experience.

It is difficult to focus on these principles and apply them to every human encounter. However, if I persist in practicing the presence of God and frequently pray to love, comfort, and understand others, I am changed. God makes me approachable, transforms me into a listener, and enables me to lovingly and effectively carry God's truth.

When I persist as described, God's Magic often permeates my human encounters.

I love you all.

August 5

Good morning.

Our keynote is "Honesty".

Today's Meditation declares feeling inadequate to be disloyalty to God.

While I understand the premise, sometimes I find it necessary to alter a valuable suggestion a bit.

I don't have the power to instantly vanquish feelings of inadequacy. Such feelings are part of the crazy picture show in my head over which I never have immediate control.

However, I believe God judges me on my behavior, not on whatever may float through my head. So, I am not disloyal to God unless I behave like a person who feels inadequate.

In fact, taking the next stitch as directed by the Divine Spark when I am fearful, doubtful, and feel inadequate is the greatest demonstration of loyalty I can make.

When I persist in loyal and trusting action, I rediscover The Magic and begin to feel loyal and trusting again.

But if I revert to demanding that I feel loyal and trusting before I will behave that way, I am again lost.

I love you all.

August 7

Good morning.

Our keynote is: "Humbly say to ourselves many times today, 'Thy will be done...'."

Today's reading refers to the spiritual principle underlying Emmett Fox's two-page pamphlet, "The Golden Key", which has pulled me out of the abyss more than anything else. It is available online with a simple search.

Just reading and learning it is of little value. It is the action it so clearly describes which will get us out of any difficulty.

Today's Meditation tells us to practice saying, "All is going to be well," which amounts to a repetitive affirmation of God's power and grace.

"The Golden Key" gives us things to repeatedly say to ourselves concerning God. By persistently doing so, we are promised success in thinking of God rather than the difficulty. We are further assured the difficulty will go away once that is accomplished.

Following Fox's clear and simple directions has magically chased hundreds of difficulties from my mind and life.

I love you all.

August 8

Good morning.

Our keynote is "Pray to seek to love, comfort, and understand..."

The Meditation for the Day tells us that the proper balance between much effort and rest will result in a successful life. In early sobriety, I went on a protracted quest for "balance".

I prayed, read, wrote inventories, and sought professional help. Balance continued to elude me.

Two or three years into my crusade for balance, I was telling a hapless AA discussion meeting ALL about it. A young man, who was only one week out of the asylum, asked simply, "If you could balance your life, Don, why couldn't you manage it?". The light finally came on!

Since that day, I have tried to keep in mind that managing or balancing my life is beyond my ability but is effortless for God.

Magically, if I simply focus on taking the next stitch as the Divine Spark directs, God balances and manages my life far better than I ever could.

I love you all.

August 9

Good morning.

Our keynote is "Help God's kids do what they need to have done".

Today's Meditation and Prayer emphasize the importance of willingness to be changed by God's grace and power.

We can and must change our behavior, one stitch at a time, but it is God who changes our minds and souls.

That principle, in my belief and experience, is the heart of AA's steps six and seven.

For years, I believed it was my mission to figure out who God wanted me to be and, with God's help, make myself into that person. I now know that my vision of an ideal me is just another self-determined objective. I am incapable of even recognizing perfection, much less attaining it.

However, when I couple acceptance that my knowledge of God's will and my power are both limited to my own next stitch with persistently trying to stitch as the Divine Spark directs, God's Magic goes to work.

The partnership of God's grace and power with my faithful stitching begins to move me toward being the person God would have me be.

I love you all.

August 10

Good morning.

Our keynote is "Persistence".

The Thought for the Day tells us that if we cooperate, God will transform our worst failures and mistakes into our greatest assets in carrying the message of hope and recovery.

In my experience, that magical process begins as soon as I make amends, set the past aside, and begin taking positive action.

Many days in sobriety, I have behaved and/or spoken badly, admitted it, and done the best I could to set it straight.

Later, in some of those very days, I have seen renewed comfort and hope in the eyes of a person with whom I shared my experience earlier in the day.

The past does not cripple me, but I can cripple myself by dwelling on the past, whether it was five minutes or 50 years ago.

If I wallow in useless and counterproductive self-recrimination, there is no magic. I am alone with my self-loathing and am of no use to God or my fellows.

I love you all.

August 11

Good morning.

Our keynote is "Courtesy".

Today's Meditation and Prayer declare God's power and grace sufficient to bring us out of our personal chaos into peace and order.

Nevertheless, my ego urges the use of my intellect to bring order into my life and find peace. History, however, shows that when I act as CEO of my life, the result is ultimately chaos, and peace is nowhere to be found.

God created and, with divine precision, orders the universe. Surely those are better qualifications for managing my life than my own dismal track record!

The only way I have found to bring God's order and peace into my life is to stitch as the Divine Spark directs. Persistently seeking to do the next right thing magically brings order and peace into my life.

I love you all.

August 12

Good morning.

Our keynote is "Gratitude".

Today's reading discusses the proper action when a person's behavior is not as we think it should be. We are told to pray for the person and then persistently behave appropriately in order to set an example.

In early sobriety, it felt like God's will for me to share my wisdom with my fellows regarding their character defects and shortcomings. Being uncertain precisely how God wanted me to set them straight, I searched the AA Big Book for directions. I could find none. In fact, there was no suggestion that I should ever tell another person what is wrong with them.

I have tried many times to explain to others what they need to correct. The ultimate result has never once been good. I now know that unsolicited advice is always criticism, no exceptions.

There is much magic in keeping my mouth shut and seeking to set an example by tending to my own behavior.

I love you all.

August 13

Good morning.

Our keynote is "Humility".

The Meditation for the Day suggests continual review and improvement of our character, which is the 10th step requirement of continuing to take personal inventory.

In early sobriety, I took this to mean that I should continually examine how I AM. That approach quickly devolved into an obsessive checking of my "spiritual temperature". I was never sure of my spiritual state or how to improve it. My efforts became just another form of useless and counterproductive obsession on self.

I was unable to change my state of being through obsessive thought of my condition.

Then I began to realize that the measure of my character is not so much how I am as it is how I behave.

This shift in angle of approach allows me to much better assess, and allow God to improve, my character. It makes the state of my character objective rather than subjective.

God did not give me the ability to clearly understand or to change the way I am. However, God did give me the power to change my behavior, one stitch at a time.

If I persistently tend to what I can DO, God magically takes care of how I AM.

I love you all.

August 14

Good morning.

Our keynote is "Honesty".

Today's reading urges us to embrace God's gift of "abundant life".

Before sobriety, I believed abundant life to be material wealth along with the praise and admiration of others. Rather than as gifts from God, I believed those things would be attained by my cleverness and effort.

Approaching life from that angle landed me in the worst kind of poverty, poverty of the spirit.

Countless times I have squandered God's precious gift of life by throwing the day back in God's face because I didn't like the way it was wrapped.

My sober experience is that the truly abundant life has little to do with the material world. It is consciousness of God and gratitude that I am a magical creature in God's Magic World for this day.

It is seeking to love, and be helpful to, my fellows instead of using them.

I pray to live today in awareness that a day of human life is a more precious gift than all the world's wealth and that life itself is abundance enough.

I love you all.

August 15

Good morning.

Our keynote is "Humbly say to ourselves many times today, 'Thy will be done',...".

Today's Meditation and Prayer emphasize our need for the fellowship of other AA members.

All spiritual fellowship reinforces faith. The AA fellowship, additionally, supports the individual's commitment to sobriety.

Another great benefit of the fellowship is its ability to expose my chronic insane thinking. My crazy ideas never present by saying, "Good morning, Don. I'm an insane idea and, while I don't care either way, I may kill you.".

Instead, they are more likely to smilingly announce, "Hi, buddy. I'm common sense.".

Sadly, my alcoholism includes a disorder of my perception which may cause me to believe and act on that lethal lie. The magic of the fellowship is that my insane ideas never sound like common sense to you, and yours never sound like common sense to me.

My mind is like a bad neighborhood; it's dangerous to go in there alone.

I love (and need) you all.

August 16

Good morning.

Our keynote is "Pray to seek to love, comfort and understand,...".

Today's Meditation and Prayer urge us to rest and find peace so we can be more effective. Stress, the great destroyer of rest, peace, and effectiveness, is usually the byproduct of my "big deals".

I was told in early sobriety that I have a disease of big deals.

My ego will grow a big deal from anything it can make about me.

My experience is that stress is unlikely unless I have made a big deal of something other than God and the 12 Steps and, therefore, made a big deal of myself.

Wildly overestimating my importance creates the illusion that I am too busy to seek spiritual sustenance, go to a meeting, or help my fellows. In reality, all three of those things magically expand time and energy by shrinking my "deals" and giving me a more realistic view of my importance.

Big deals are a cancer on my soul.

I love you all.

August 17

Good morning.

Our keynote is: "Help God's kids do what they need to have done".

The 24 Hour Book's Prayer for the Day asks that I may live in the sunshine of God's Spirit and be energized by it.

There are "gray times" in my sobriety when I am unable to feel or see the spiritual sunshine and feel lost in a fog of my doubt and fear. Then my brain drives me further into the fog by THINKING about it.

I make little progress by merely thinking about my plight and praying for God to lift the fog so I can act.

Far better results come from asking for the strength to take the next stitch as directed, DESPITE my negative feelings. When I couple that prayer with behaving like one who feels the faith, the fog begins to lift.

I am not transported back to God's Magic by thoughts and prayers alone. I rediscover it by WALKING through the fog back into the sunshine, one divinely guided step at a time.

Thank God for the realization that I don't have to feel right in order to behave correctly!

I love you all.

August 18

Good morning.

Our keynote is "Persistence".

Today's Meditation and Prayer tell us that the quality of our relationship with God cannot be divorced from our treatment of God's children.

The theme reinforces my experience and belief that interaction with others is my only tangible interaction with God.

What I do unto others, I also do unto God.

Today's theme also brings to mind the spiritual power of simple courtesy. I have come to believe that no spiritual principle is more important, and that it is impossible to be spiritual and discourteous at the same time.

By persistently seeking to be courteous to everyone I encounter, I make great progress toward loving, comforting, and understanding my fellows.

By the progress in my human relations, I am drawn closer to God.

There is much magic in courtesy. There is never an acceptable excuse for me to abandon it.

I love you all.

August 19

Good morning.

Our keynote is "Courtesy".

Today's reading defines worship as consciousness of God's divine majesty.

We are told that worship will infuse us with divine power, love, and healing.

I agree, but believe the power, love, and healing to be only tools which assist us in the real purpose of worship.

It is like a servant or employee being provided with the things needed to do the employer's work.

Merely admiring God, while acknowledging the Divine Power and Grace, is essential and certainly brings great gifts, but, for me, it is only the foundation of worship.

My worship gains substance and reality when I use its fruits to get about our divine purpose of loving God's kids and helping them do what they need to have done.

Awareness of God's divinity and majesty, when coupled with my persistent, divinely guided useful action, summons God's Magic.

I worship and honor God more effectively with my feet than with my mind and mouth.

I love you all.

August 20

Good morning.

Our keynote is "Gratitude".

Today's Meditation and Prayer warn us against morbid reflection on the past.

My first sponsor, Cherry, repeatedly told me that the single most useless and counterproductive of all human endeavors is self-recrimination. It accomplishes nothing positive and cripples me in my efforts to do the next right thing and be helpful to my fellows.

Of course, I must do what I can to set right the wreckage of my past and promptly admit and amend my ongoing mistakes and failures. But, beyond such corrective action, I need to stay out of the past.

I must also remain aware that five seconds ago is just as much the past as 50 years ago.

The only place and time I can find God is here and now.

If I go into the past, I go alone and without God's Magic.

Today I pray to stay out of the past and live in the moment where I am armored, strengthened and guided by God's power and grace.

I love you all.

August 21

Good morning.

Our keynote is "Humility".

Today's reading urges us to loosen our grip on all things of this earth.

The same spiritual principle is referenced by the AA Third Step Prayer in asking that we be relieved of the "bondage of self".

I was bewildered when first told that "the bondage of self" means my relationships, my children, my health, my finances, my reputation, etc.

I now know that I am not asking for those people and things to be taken away.

I am asking to realize they do not belong to me, but are a day-to-day loan from God.

Realizing my role to be caretaker for this day only, rather than owner, relieves me of the burden of constantly scrambling to obtain and maintain MY relationships and things.

It enables me to better love, tend and enjoy the dear people and things which God allows me to have just for today.

I find The Magic in having daily loans from God, rather than possessing relationships, situations, and things.

I love you all.

August 22

Good morning.

Our keynote is "Humility".

The Thought for the Day asks if I am completely honest with myself and others.

Honesty with others is far more objective than self-honesty. I know when I deceive others, but whether I deceive myself is always subject to debate.

Of course, I can and must maintain self-honesty on basic issues such as the fact that I can never drink successfully.

Also, the 12 steps are by far the most successful route to self-candor I have found, and I must persistently use and apply them every day.

However, obsessing on self-honesty has proved to be just another form of my impotent self-obsession.

If I live the Steps and diligently try to stitch as the Divine Spark directs, I believe God, magically, makes me self-honest enough.

Less than perfect thoughts accompanying right action no more invalidate good behavior than my grand intentions and rationalizations excuse bad behavior.

What goes on in my head never leaves a footprint on reality.

If I persist in doing the right thing, the world, and, I believe, God care little about the crazy pictures show in my head.

I love you all.

August 23

Good morning.

Our keynote is "Honesty".

Today's reading cautions us not to let the small trials and vexations of the day overwhelm us. Surrender in the face of truly significant difficulties is, ironically, often easier than accepting my powerlessness over little things.

My original sponsor frequently pointed out my tendency to "pole vault over mouse droppings". He also diagnosed me as having a "Chicken Little complex". An acorn falls on my head and I think the sky is falling.

Regardless of the size and nature of the difficulty, I need to persistently accept that my knowledge of God's will and my actual power are extremely limited. Both go no further than my own very next action.

It is by focusing on my next right stitch, instead of fretting about the "big picture", that I accept the reality of what I can and can't do.

In turn, my action-based acceptance opens the channel for God's Magic to deal with my difficulties, large and small.

I love you all.

August 24

Good morning.

Our keynote is: "Humbly say to ourselves many times today, 'Thy will be done',..."

Today's Meditation tells us that it is possible for God to change our way of living.

Before sobriety, I tried on my own to identify and bring about the needed changes in my life.

It didn't work.

For the first nine years I was sober, I tried to do the same thing, but with God's help. To my surprise and frustration, that didn't work much better.

In May of 1990, I began to take an entirely different view of steps six and seven. I began to realize that I cannot effectively work on any of my character defects just as I could not effectively work on my alcoholism.

For the last 32 years, I have sought to come to God as a little child, giving up the idea that I can determine what changes need to be made or how to bring them about.

I have sought to focus on the Divine Spark's guidance one stitch at a time, rather than trying to figure out who I should be.

I have done that very imperfectly, but persistently, and God has magically changed my way of living and my life in wonderful ways.

I love you all.

August 25

Good morning.

Our keynote is: "Pray to seek to love, comfort and understand, ..."

The Prayer for the Day asks that I may not speak or act in the midst of emotional upheaval but wait until the tempest is past.

Looking back over my lifetime, for every one time I regret having not spoken or acted, there are countless regrets over fearful, angry, hasty, or "cute" words and actions.

In the legal world, the general wisdom is, "The less you say, the less trouble you will have".

When I am tempted by emotional disturbance to speak or act rashly, my most effective tool is the Prayer of St. Francis. If I will run, "...seek to love, comfort, and understand," through my mind, over and over, I am far less likely to damage or destroy relationships.

Furthermore, if I will remind myself that courtesy is always appropriate, it will prevent much conflict and bitterness. I am also well advised to follow my old sponsor's advice and keep my mouth shut and be still when I am uncertain what to say or do. Silence is not only golden, it is often magic.

I love you all.

August 26

Good morning.

Our keynote is "Help God's kids do what they need to have done."

The Meditation and Prayer for the Day emphasize obeying the laws of nature and God. They, like my first sponsor, hold that we get the divinely perfect consequences of our actions. Whether I am useful, successful, peaceful, and in harmony with God and my fellows on any given day depends on what I do, not on my understanding.

Contemplating and studying God's law is a noble endeavor and can enhance my ability to live a spiritual life. However, if I am to have a spiritual life, it will be the result of behaving in accordance with the Divine Spark, one stitch at a time. The Spark is a far better guide than my brain. If I am attuned to and heed it, I will follow God's law, even if I don't intellectually understand it. "The spiritual life is not a theory. We have to live it."

For me, the Divine Spark, which is the little piece of God inside each of us, IS The Magic.

I love you all.

August 27

Good morning.

Our keynote is "Persistence."

Today's Meditation and Prayer declare the grace of God to be the only solution to disharmony and disorder in human relationships.

Bringing the grace of God (i.e., The Divine Third) into my human relations requires a dramatic reversal of my old angle of approach. Before sobriety, my objective was generally to procure love, comfort, and understanding from everyone I encountered. Harmonious and orderly relationships are only possible by overcoming my ego's demands in that regard.

The most effective action I have found is silently and repetitively praying, before and during each human encounter, to lay aside whether I am loved, comforted, or understood and seek, instead, to give those things to my fellows. That shift of focus so profoundly changes the dynamics that it seems to sprinkle angel dust on human encounters.

For decades, the silent repetition of that prayer has proved to be nothing short of magic in my relations with others. It works. It really does!

I love you all.

August 28

Good morning.

Our keynote is "Courtesy."

The Meditation for the Day tells us that happiness cannot be achieved if it is our objective; it comes only as a byproduct of love and service.

Before sobriety, my primary objective in life was my own happiness. That angle of approach resulted in emptiness, chaos, and profound unhappiness.

Since embarking on the AA path, I have, very imperfectly, stumbled in the direction of trying to bring love, comfort, and understanding to my fellows rather than trying to make myself happy.

My brain and ego still grumble that I should put myself first, but the Divine Spark leads me, one stitch at a time, to seek to help God's kids do what they need to have done.

The results have been far better. When I seek to serve God's kids instead of my selfishness, I often get to enjoy the magic of happiness until self once again gains control.

When that happens, I must persistently return to God's guidance and seeking to help my fellows until rightness is restored and happiness again visits me.

I love you all.

August 29

Good morning.

Our keynote is "Gratitude."

Today's Meditation declares the two great divine gifts to be God's Spirit and the power of choice. God's Spirit (i.e., the Divine Spark) provides my only true glimpse of God's will. That glimpse is only in the right now and illuminates only my single next stitch.

The power of choice is much of our humanity, but, like the Divine Spark, it is limited to the present instant and is only available for my very next action.

In early sobriety, I thought I had made a decision to follow God's will when I formed and stated that intention. I now know that an intention is not a decision. It will only grow into a decision if I begin to act on it.

My intention to follow the path of spirituality accomplished nothing until I began to walk the path. So, rather than exercising the Divinely given power of choice one dramatic and life-changing time, I must exercise it many times each day with every single stitch.

I form intentions with my brain but make decisions with my feet.

As always, persistent action is my path to The Magic.

I love you all.

August 30

Good morning.

Our keynote is "Honesty."

Today's Meditation and Prayer promise abundant life if we embrace the divine paradox: "The more we give, the more we have."

We are cautioned against allowing mean or selfish thoughts to stand in the way of our giving.

There are always times when I feel obsessed with myself and/or empty of anything positive to give to others.

I have found that saying a silent prayer and seeking to give, despite selfishness or feeling spiritually empty, brings about two miracles.

First, I am often told that things I said or did grudgingly, or while feeling spiritually bankrupt, were of great value to others.

Second, when I make myself give, even though I don't want to do so or feel I have anything to offer, I soon discover that my own spirit has been renewed.

It works like magic.

I believe we are never more spiritual than when we seek to give despite wanting to be selfish or feeling spiritually bankrupt.

I love you all.

August 31

Good morning.

Our keynote is: "Humbly say to ourselves many times today, 'Thy will be done'...".

Today's reading holds that avoiding judgment and criticism, while building up others instead of tearing them down, will enhance our ability to be helpful.

In my experience, a good starting point in helpfulness is reminding myself that unsolicited advice is always criticism. No exceptions.

Next, I should seek to give my entire interest, attention, and love to the person in front of me.

Of course, praying to love, comfort, and understand is always a pathway to harmony.

Finally, it's hard to overestimate the power of simple courtesy. If I am mindful of courtesy, I won't make critical or judgmental statements or expressions, and people will be much more open to any message I may carry.

It is impossible for me to be discourteous and spiritual at the same time.

Like the Prayer of St. Francis, courtesy is magic in human relations. It is love in action, and love moves mountains.

I love you all.

SEPTEMBER

September 1

Good morning.

Our keynote is "Persistence."

Today's reading declares the basis of an effective and comfortable life to be the willingness to believe and behave as if God is everything.

The AA Big Book describes the inevitable moment when each alcoholic must choose whether God is everything or God is nothing.

I first chose to believe God is everything many years ago. Some blessed and joyful days, I feel certain I am securely cradled in the hands of a loving and all-powerful God.

Other days, mentally, my faith is weak, and I may feel I am struggling alone against a hostile universe. On those days, I must reaffirm my choice that God is everything. My temporarily failed intention to believe can be made a decision again by behaving as one who knows God to be everything.

The action IS the decision. When I make that choice with my feet, God magically restores my mind to knowing and feeling that God is, indeed, everything.

I love you all.

September 2

Good morning.

Our keynote is "Courtesy."

Today's reading urges us to stand aside and not interfere with the working of God's Spirit through us.

When I approach any human encounter with an agenda to manipulate and be loved, comforted, and understood, it creates stress and rarely works. When I let go of my agenda and pray silently to speak the quiet, loving truth and seek to love, comfort, and understand, the results are blessed. Stress and self-interest are replaced by peace and love. The interaction becomes more comfortable and productive for all involved.

In the years I practiced law prior to sobriety, I would have scoffed at the idea of such an approach working better than my self-proclaimed clever brain and tongue. My sober experience is that God's way is nothing short of magic in ALL my human encounters, personal and professional.

I have learned that the quiet, loving truth is the loudest, most effective sound on earth, inside or outside of a courtroom.

Following God's guidance, a stitch at a time, makes me a better sponsor, spouse, father, friend, lawyer, etc., than I could dream of becoming on my own.

I love you all.

September 3

Good morning.

Our keynote is "Gratitude."

Today's reading reminds us that, while we cannot directly see God, our spiritual life depends on maintaining consciousness that God dwells in ourselves and others.

I daily refer to "God's Magic" in my comments. My purpose in doing so is to keep me aware that we are all magical creatures in God's Magic World. It helps me focus on the miracle of being a living human being in God's exquisitely created and functioning universe.

When I have that in mind, I will feel God in you and in me. I will not throw the priceless gift of a day of human life back in God's face because I don't like the wrapping. I will treat my fellows like the magical children of God they are instead of tools to use for or obstacles to my selfish ends. When aware of The Magic of being a living human for a day, I don't take being alive or the people around me for granted.

In that awareness, I view my life, the world, and the people in it with reverent awe. My angle of approach toward the world and all God's magical creatures is transformed.

I love you all.

September 4

Good morning.

Our keynote is "Humility."

The Prayer for the Day asks that I may have a mission of conciliation and do the things that make for peace. My prayers to that end are answered only when I follow them with action. Some of my most effective tools for promoting peace with my fellows, and within myself, are as follows:

1. Avoid trying to make others think I am right.
2. Never give unsolicited advice. It is always received as criticism.
3. Don't look for or expect personal slights or criticism. If I am looking for them I will find them in abundance.
4. Repeatedly pray to love, comfort, and understand.
5. Focus on the feelings and needs of others rather than my own.
6. Be unfailingly courteous.
7. Don't have big deals, regardless of how important my ego wants me to believe things are.
8. Leave policing and judging to those who are paid to do so.

Prayer, coupled with employing those tools, brings the magic of peace and conciliation.

I love you all.

September 5

Good morning.

Our keynote is "Honesty."

Today's Meditation urges us to try to see more of the beauty, truth, knowledge, and power around us. I believe that is so important because if we are to be part of the good in the world, we must see that good.

I am reminded of Dr. Paul O.'s story in the Big Book. He talks about his "magic magnifying mind," meaning that focusing on either the good or bad will cause either to grow. What we do not dwell on tends to fade toward nothingness.

If I persistently focus on the negativity in the world, a situation, or a person, that negativity will grow until it completely eclipses the positive. Gratefully, it also works the other way around. Today, I pray to focus my "magic magnifying mind" on the good in the world and in each person and situation I encounter.

The more I look for, think about, and talk about the good, the better chance I have of behaving in such a way as to be part of it today.

I love you all.

September 6

Good morning.

Our keynote is "Humbly say to ourselves many times each day, 'Thy will be done',...".

The Thought for the Day discusses the AA motto, "Live and Let Live."

That principle is crucial to my relations with others and my own peace and serenity.

When feeling agitated or aggrieved, I have often found peace and sanity by asking myself three questions about the disturbing situation and/or person:

1. What is another person's business?
2. What is God's business?
3. What is my business?

If my disturbance persists, I write about whose business the disturbing circumstances are.

Upon examining the finished product, it is always shocking how little is my business!

That process brings me down to size and frees me to live and let live.

My first sponsor often called a pen and paper a recovered alcoholic's best friends. Identifying and minding only my own business produces magical results!

I love you all.

September 7

Good morning.

Our keynote is: "Pray to seek to love, comfort, and understand..."

Today's Meditation and Prayer counsel us to look only to God for security.

I have wasted much of my life chasing the myth of human security. I now realize there is no such thing. All the world's wealth and power can't guarantee my next breath or the continued life or love of a dear one. Worldly events beyond my control can strip me of material wealth, power, and acclaim at any time. Even if I seem to hold onto the world's bounty, in the end, it is all forfeit to death. However, if I maintain consciousness of The Divine, and rely only on God, I live in comfort and security. From that angle of approach, acceptance of the fragile and fleeting nature of all things human actually enhances my gratitude and appreciation for the day. Just for today, God has bestowed on me the priceless gift of being a magic creature in God's Magic World.

I pray not to squander a minute of today fretting about a few unwelcome details.

I love you all.

September 8

Good morning.

Our keynote is: "Help God's kids do what they need to have done".

Today's reading emphasizes maintaining gratitude and consciousness of God's love.

Gratitude brings God's love to my conscious mind, and then awareness of the magnitude of God's love fosters even greater gratitude.

My core gratitude needs to be for the gift of a day of human life; for being part of The Magic today.

It is closely followed by gratitude for sobriety, without which I would have no life.

Then there are the circumstances of my birth and life. It wasn't merit that brought about my normal birth in middle-class America instead of being born in a third-world hovel with profound physical and mental handicaps.

It is ALL by the grace of God.

It is embarrassing that I ever harbor or express any complaint about my life. When I slip into the madness of self-pity, continuing to behave gratefully restores sanity.

Today, I pray to behave as gratefully as I surely should feel.

I love you all.

September 9

Good morning.

Our keynote is "Persistence".

Today's Meditation and Prayer continue emphasizing consciousness of, and reliance upon, God.

It requires little effort or sacrifice on my part to rely on God when my intellectual faith is strong and I am able to see the glorious results of faith and trust in The Divine.

However, there are times when it is difficult for me to realize God, see the bounty flowing from faith, or maintain intellectual confidence in the Divine Spark's guidance.

Gratefully, when hampered by feeble faith, if I persist in stumbling forward by taking the next stitch as the Spark directs, my mind begins to clear and my soul begins to calm.

That magic will not happen as long as I sit in paralysis, waiting for God to set my mind and feelings aright.

God requires me to act while still doubtful and fearful, which I believe to be the most profound and effective faith I can exhibit.

When I act, the divine partnership of God's power and grace with my right action magically restores me to sanity, faith, peace, and wholeness.

I love you all.

September 10

Good morning.

Our keynote is "Courtesy".

Today's Meditation and Prayer discuss the satisfaction derived from prioritizing serving God over self-interest.

Almost all my opportunities to serve God involve serving others. In fact, I find it impossible to separate the two. I find little clarity on how to directly serve God's needs or desires. The needs of God's children, however, are often painfully clear.

My fellows are the only tangible manifestation of God with which I can interact. I believe that what I do for or against God's children, I also do for or against God.

Part of The Divine Paradox is that my worldly well-being is better served as a byproduct of helping God's children than by making self-interest my first priority.

If I maintain awareness of God and seek to act as guided by the Divine Spark, my behavior will magically serve my fellows, my God, and as a byproduct, myself.

I love you all.

September 11

Good morning.

Our keynote is "Gratitude".

Today's reading declares God to be the source of our strength, love, and peace. After two years of regular exposure to AA and mentally struggling to believe in a Higher Power, I was unable to open my mind to belief or stay sober. I was on the precipice of a mad dog, alcoholic death.

Then a simple and obvious realization came to me. It proved to be the key that finally opened my mind to belief and faith in God. My epiphany sprang from casually thinking of the Biblical phrase, "God is Love". Having always been interested in language, it occurred to me that if God is Love, then necessarily, Love IS God. I had no problem accepting Love as my Higher Power. That breakthrough prompted me to begin behaving as one who trusts and relies on God. Magically, my imperfect but persistent faithful behavior, despite lingering doubt, triggered a miracle. It became the basis of my transformation from a hopeless and helpless alcoholic to a happy, joyous, and free child of God.

I love you all.

September 12

Good morning.

Our keynote is "Humility".

Today's Meditation declares striving to attune one's will to the will of God to be the most important thing in life. I agree, and it is also the essence of AA's third step. Newly sober and beginning to realize the need to serve God, I believed it necessary to figure out God's objectives so I could use my understanding to further them. That approach proved ineffective, frustrating, and, in the end, counterproductive.

Finally, I began to realize that I have less chance of understanding God's overall will or objectives than a chimpanzee does of mastering quantum physics. The only glimpse of God's will I ever see is for my own very next action, and the only power I ever have is over that next action. Happily, that has proved to be knowledge and power enough.

Like Thomas Merton, I don't know what pleases God in the big picture, but I believe my Higher Power is pleased by my stumbling efforts to please God with each single stitch.

The magic of attuning my will to God's is in heeding the Divine Spark's guidance, one stitch at a time.

I love you all.

September 13

Good morning.

Our keynote is "Honesty".

The Meditation for the Day declares that the spirit of prayer can alter an atmosphere from one of discord to one of reconciliation. I have experienced that phenomenon countless times in sobriety. In a disagreement with a loved one, a heated atmosphere in a courtroom, a chance encounter gone awry, or any other discordant situation, the Prayer of St. Francis has never failed me. By silently praying to seek to love, comfort, and understand the others involved, rather than being concerned with my self-interest and how I am perceived, I have often felt the heat and tension in the room drop dramatically. Repetition of the prayer before and during human interaction summons the Divine Third, which transforms everything. Love, courtesy, and mutual understanding replace ill feeling, fear, and sarcasm. "Magic" is no overstatement of the prayer's impact on my human relations.

I love you all.

September 14

Good morning.

Our keynote is: "Humbly say to ourselves many times today, 'Thy will be done,...'"

The Meditation for the Day quotes a prayer which, in essence, says, "We believe. Please help our unbelief". That prayer, which I pray at least every morning and night, implicitly acknowledges the impossibility of constantly maintaining thoughts, feelings, and beliefs of perfect faith. The inevitable doubts do not mean that my faith has failed. My faith does not fail unless or until I fail, or refuse, to behave faithfully. I cannot control the old crazy picture show in my head, and I don't believe God judges me on anything beyond my control. However, I have been given power over my next action. I believe both God and the world judge me only on how I exercise that power. As long as I seek to make my next stitch consistent with faith, my state of mind is ultimately irrelevant. It impacts only my comfort, not reality. In fact, I believe behaving faithfully, while feeling doubtful and fearful, is the most spiritually valuable thing I can do. Magically, persistent faithful stitching, when plagued by doubt and fear, returns me to the comfort and peace of faithful thoughts, feelings, and beliefs.

I love you all.

September 15

Good morning.

Our keynote is: "Pray to seek to love, comfort and understand, ..."

The Thought for the Day quotes the AA Big Book, stating, "We all realize that we know only a little. God will constantly disclose more to all of us". The quote reinforces my conviction that I am incapable of foreseeing or understanding the patterns of my life. The wording, "...constantly disclose more", I believe, refers to the fact that my only glimpse of God's will is for my own next stitch. God does, indeed, light my path, but only for one step at a time with a penlight, never with a floodlight. For me, the essence of faith is taking the single lighted step while blind to the rest of the path. My friend and sponsor, Bob B., says life is lived forward, but only understood backward. I never see or understand the tapestry of my life as it unfolds, but, in looking back, I see the beauty and perfection of God's patterns. It's magic!

I love you all.

September 16

Good morning.

Our keynote is: "Help God's kids do what they need to have done..."

Today's reading suggests that spiritual work may be eternal. It then directs us to pray to give freely to all who ask for help.

Since childhood, I have been told that the only thing we take out of this world is what we have done for others. In my sober years, I have come to absolutely believe it.

However, helping God's kids only in hopes of some heavenly reward is self-robbery. As Chuck C. said, it is barter and will deny us the spirituality, peace, and happiness in this world which results from helping God's kids for fun and for free because we want to. Living life for myself is an enticing idea which my ego constantly promotes. The problem is, I tried it for 37 years and it simply does not work. It ultimately led to emptiness, despair, and chaos.

I touch The Magic through seeking to help others for fun and for free, not by struggling to serve my own selfish ends.

I love you all.

September 17

Good morning.

Our keynote is "Persistence".

The Meditation for the Day states that following spiritual laws will generally produce happiness, but disobeying them will inevitably bring unhappiness.

My original sponsor, Cherry, used different words to convey that same truth. He believed we get the divinely perfect consequences of our actions. No amount of prayer, knowledge, or good intentions, he taught, can overcome the following rule:

The only route to comfort is doing things which ultimately make one comfortable and ceasing to do things which ultimately make one uncomfortable.

No barter. No exceptions.

I sometimes wish Cherry had been less than 100% correct on that point, but experience has proved him absolutely right.

I can't access The Magic by cutting corners. That door is unlocked only by my persistent behavior consistent with faith and love.

I love you all.

September 18

Good morning.

Our keynote is "Courtesy".

The Thought for the Day declares belief in a Power greater than ourselves to be the fundamental basis of AA. A "venture of belief" is the foundation of most efforts to live a spiritual life, and "venture" is the ideal word to describe my sobriety and spiritual journey.

Like explorers throughout history, when I embarked on my venture I couldn't foresee the obstacles to be encountered or the discoveries to be made. However, by persistently taking one action consistent with faith after another, I actually came to believe and continue to find a greater and more profound faith. I find God with my feet more than with my mind. Along the way, I make exciting discoveries and reap great rewards. My venture has no known destination other than the journey itself.

As I stumble on, one stitch at a time, with the Divine Spark as my compass, glimpses of The Magic become more frequent, more lasting, and more clear.

I love you all.

September 19

Good morning.

Our keynote is "Gratitude".

The Meditation for the Day promises that living according to spiritual laws will bring our share of joy, peace, satisfaction, and success. Even after awakening to the need for spirituality, I initially viewed it as somehow apart from the details and reality of living a successful material life. Nothing has changed and enriched my life more than realizing that the spiritual and material are interwoven in the tapestry of my life.

If I persist in trying to heed the Divine Spark, one stitch at a time, my material well-being is also served. The truth and simplicity of that angle of approach is offensive to my ego. It screams that surely, I must outthink, outperform, and outmaneuver my fellows in order to satisfy my material needs and desires. Nevertheless, the facts are that walking the spiritual path, although imperfectly and haltingly, has proven to be magic in every single area of my life, including the material.

I love you all.

September 20

Good morning.

Our keynote is "Humility".

The Thought for the Day stresses the need for personal inventory. Being "... absolutely honest with ourselves and others" is emphasized. I agree, as long as my honesty with others is always tempered with compassion, courtesy, and discretion. Otherwise, it is not really honesty but a form of hostility. There are a few absolutes about being honest with myself. As an alcoholic, the prime example is total acceptance of my inability to drink alcohol successfully.

However, I must be careful not to let my quest for self-honesty descend into self-psychoanalysis. If I fall into that pit, it becomes just another way to obsess on myself. Because the basis of my alcoholism is self-centeredness, I cannot effectively treat it with any form of self-obsession. It's like trying to put out a fire with gasoline.

If I accept my own limitations and am rigorously but compassionately honest with others, self-honesty magically seems to take care of itself.

I love you all.

September 21

Good morning.

Our keynote is "Honesty".

The Prayer for the Day asks that we be freed from intellectual pride. I was a prisoner of that especially lethal form of the first deadly sin. Intellectual arrogance drove the total destruction of my life and then blocked me from God and recovery.

I believe my life was saved when I was told that nobody is too dumb for AA, but the ones like me who think they are too smart are regularly buried. To live and be sober, I had to begin behaving like a person who does not lean on their understanding. I had to start doing things consistent with faith, despite my thoughts, feelings, and beliefs to the contrary. I began trying to come as a trusting little child and use my brain to do God's will and help God's kids.

I'm not capable of understanding God's overall will and I have no power beyond my own next action, but I can seek to obey the Divine Spark one stitch at a time. Persistently trying to do so turned out to be, literally, all my God requires of me! On my better days, it is that simple.

I love you all.

September 22

Good morning.

Our keynote is: "Humbly say to ourselves many times today, 'Thy will be done'...".

Today's Meditation promises us great rewards for continuing to behave faithfully, despite the apparent wrongness of our circumstances.

Many years ago, I talked with a man who had, for a long time, successfully made a living playing poker in Las Vegas. Having known some people who failed spectacularly at that endeavor, I asked how he managed to succeed.

He said the difference between success and failure has little to do with the good hands; anyone can play them heroically. In the end, he claimed, the most important factor is how you play the hands that are so bad you don't even want to look at them. I don't play poker, but applying that principle to everything, spiritual and material, has produced magical results! People have told me that I helped them most when I felt spiritually bankrupt while working with them.

Apparent professional disasters have, instead, turned out to be my most satisfying material successes.

I pray today to give my entire interest, attention, and love to the very worst "hands" I am dealt.

I love you all.

September 23

Our keynote is: "Pray to seek to love, comfort, and understand...".

When faced with a problem beyond our strength, today's Meditation directs us to turn to God by an ACT of faith.

In my experience, God frequently requires action on my part prior to removing a burden.

Many years ago, an AA member asked me, "Don, do you know how we turn a toothache over to God?" Of course, the answer is, "We go to a dentist." Praying, going to meetings, and talking with my sponsor haven't helped my toothaches much.

I was also told that if I am hungry, locking myself in a closet and praying for food is not likely to result in a hotdog squirting through the keyhole.

My God will do almost anything for me, but will usually do nothing without my cooperation.

The magic is in the partnership of God's power and grace with my action.

I love you all.

September 24

Good morning.

Our keynote is: "Help God's kids do what they need to have done...".

The Prayer for the Day asks that we may follow the "dictates of our conscience" and the "inner urging of the soul".

I believe both terms refer to what I call the "Divine Spark".

Hard experience has taught me that persistently ignoring or willfully refusing to follow Divine guidance extinguishes any hope of comfort or peace.

Worldly success, seemingly won by my departure from the Divine Spark's guidance, has ultimately been empty. It has often brought more heartache than it was worth.

Whether I choose to call it the Divine Spark, conscience, "moral compass," or "Holy Spirit," etc., the truth and what is right remain constant.

To live as a peaceful and joyful magical creature in God's Magic World, I must realize and seek to follow my Creator's stitch-by-stitch directions.

I love you all.

September 25

Good morning.

Our keynote is "Courtesy."

Today's Meditation and Prayer urge us to express our gratitude to God by viewing ourselves as servants of God's other children.

If everyone on earth approached life seeking to be a tireless servant to all their sisters and brothers, we would live in paradise. When I live with that perspective, the minuscule bit of love and light created may have no visible impact on the overall world. However, seeking to live as a servant to my fellows transforms my personal world. I become more conscious of the fact that I am a happy, joyous, and free magical creature living in God's Magic World. The peace and happiness, which I frantically and vainly sought by trying to force the world to serve my ends, is freely given when I am a servant to all around me. It is one more example of both the Divine Paradox and enlightened self-interest.

I love you all.

September 26

Good morning.

Our keynote is "Gratitude".

Today's reading, like AA's 11th Step, emphasizes maintaining conscious contact with our Higher Power. We sustain and improve our awareness of God, in part, through prayer and meditation in the morning and before retiring.

Where I get in trouble is with the other 95% of the day.

With life coming at me from all directions, it's easy to lose any thought of God or spirituality.

I find my solution in following the 11th Step's simple instructions by pausing when agitated or doubtful and asking for the right thought or action, constantly reminding myself that I am no longer running the show, and humbly saying to myself many times throughout the day, "Thy will be done".

The Big Book then promises that I will be much more efficient, not tire so easily, and be in much less danger of excitement, fear, anger, worry, self-pity, or foolish decisions.

Magically, it is that simple, and it works. It really does!

I love you all.

September 27

Good morning.

Our keynote is "Persistence".

The Thought for the Day examines the term "spiritual experience" as discussed in AA's Big Book. The 12th Step begins with the phrase, "Having had a spiritual awakening as the result of these steps...". The only change ever made in the basic text was to substitute the word "awakening" for "experience". The change was made because relatively few AA members claim a sudden and dramatic spiritual experience similar to Bill W's. I have never had such an experience, but the action of living the Steps has indeed awakened me to the fact that I am a spiritual creature in a spiritual world.

Any spirituality developed in me came gradually and as the result of many "stitches" consistent with spirituality. Thank God, Bill was prompted to action by his spiritual experience. However, my spiritual awakening came as the result of action consistent with spirituality.

As always, I find The Magic by first taking action. Waiting for a spiritual experience to prompt me to action would have left me in a pauper's grave decades ago. "The spiritual life is not a theory. We have to live it". If you want to know whether I am spiritual, don't ask me; I could not give you a valid response. Instead, watch me over time and you will know for sure.

I love you all.

September 28

Good morning.

Our keynote is "Humility".

The Thought for the Day suggests that we alcoholics continue to pay close attention to the Big Book. I am reminded of my first sponsor's frequent declaration that he was going to get into all the other recovery, psychological, and spiritual readings... as soon as he mastered the Big Book! Of course, he never mastered the Big Book.

He wasn't discouraging spiritual seeking, nor was he disparaging other recovery and spiritual writings. He was urging me to keep it simple and teaching that simplicity strengthens spirituality and over-complication threatens it. He was underscoring that all intellectual and psychological approaches to alcoholic recovery have ultimately failed.

He likened constant flirtation with numerous outside writings, instead of fully utilizing the Big Book, to standing on a whale's back while fishing for minnows!

I find The Magic through simplicity and action, never by intellectual gymnastics.

I love you all.

September 29

Good morning.

Our keynote is "Honesty".

The Meditation for the Day promises we can effectively discharge our responsibilities if we ask God each day for the necessary strength.

God has never failed to provide the strength and power I need to deal with today. However, God has never once given me the strength to deal with tomorrow. That help only comes when tomorrow becomes today.

Also, I have found that while God provides the required strength, my fear and reluctance are not necessarily removed. It works better for me to ask for the strength to do what must be done DESPITE my fear and reluctance than to implore God to make it feel easy for me.

When I partner with God by adding my action, however reluctantly and fearfully, to God's power and grace, something magic happens. I begin to resemble a responsible, effective, and useful human being.

I love you all.

September 30

Good morning.

Our keynote is: "Humbly say to ourselves many times today, 'Thy will be done',...".

The Meditation for the Day declares that contact with God renews our courage. Before sobriety, I measured everything by my feelings rather than reality. Therefore, I believed courage to be the absence of fear. I had it backwards. The truth is, the greater the fear, the more courageous the action. Today my favorite definition of "courage" is, "Doing the right thing when I don't want to do it". In fact, if fear is removed, then courage is no longer necessary because fear has been replaced by confidence. I have come to view courage as action in the face of fear, not a state of mind.

God gives me the strength to deal with whatever is before me right now. However, it is only AFTER I behave courageously that fear is magically replaced by confidence.

I love you all.

OCTOBER

October 1

Good morning.

Our keynote is "Pray to seek to love, comfort and understand..."

The Thought for the Day asks if we are letting self-consciousness or fear interfere with our ability to be helpful and effective. We are told that self-consciousness is pride.

I have also long believed "embarrassment" to be just a long synonym for "ego."

When focused on the impression I am making, I usually don't make a very good impression.

It would be impossible to overstate the positive impact on my life of persistently and repetitively praying to seek to love, comfort, and understand, rather than to be loved, comforted, and understood.

The same is true of praying to give my entire interest, attention and love to whomever or whatever is immediately in front of me.

Silently, and very frequently, saying those two prayers brings harmony and peace to my human relations and effectiveness to my endeavors in every area of life.

When focusing on others, self-consciousness, fear, conflict, and frantic ineffective activity are magically replaced by unselfishness, harmony, and effectiveness.

It's so simple and it works so well.

I love you all.

October 2

Good morning.

Our keynote is: "Help God's kids do what they need to have done,..."

The Prayer for the Day asks that I may have a yielded will which is attuned to the will of God.

Prior to a spiritual awakening as the result of the 12 Steps, I had many things backwards. Yielding my will looked like the ultimate weakness and seeking to do God's will seemed a lunatic fringe flirtation with the occult.

Humility felt like a character defect and I counted a strong self-will as my greatest asset. My arrogance eventually plunged me into spiritual, moral, and material bankruptcy. I became a shivering denizen of King Alcohol's mad realm.

A loving, and extremely forgiving, God gave me the great gift of beginning to follow directions, even though I did not want to, did not understand or agree with them or believe they would work.

My persistent stumbling in the right direction, coupled with God's grace and power, transformed and continues to transform me into awareness that we are magical creatures living in God's Magic World. Living in God's Magic, rather than shivering in King Alcohol's mad realm, is the difference between heaven and hell.

I love you all.

October 3

Good morning.

The Thought for the Day urges us to cultivate an optimistic and encouraging attitude toward newcomers in AA. That angle of approach has borne great fruit in ALL my human encounters. If I look for and expect the worst in someone, that is what I am likely to find.

However, if I look past the negative judgments of the crazy picture show in my head and approach the actions and characteristics which offend me with love and tolerance, magic happens.

Those my mind initially judged as obnoxious, selfish, and dishonest are often transformed into magical children of God, struggling to do the best they can. Sometimes they become treasured and trusted friends. Love not only changes me, it transforms all those around me.

If God is Love, then necessarily, Love is God.

And, I love you all.

October 4

Good morning.
Our keynote is "Persistence".

Today's Meditation and Prayer are about the peace, joy and power which flow from a truly calm spirit.

Sandy B., frequently declared that he always wanted to be the least disturbed person in the room. Adopting Sandy's goal has benefited me greatly.

Prayer, meditation and maintaining awareness of God are essential for a calm spirit.

But, there are also some things I must avoid. At the top of the list is "big deals". When I make a big deal out of anything that is not God or the 12 steps, I am really making a big deal out of me. Calmness and big deals are mutually exclusive. Big deals foster excitement, fear, ego and frantic activity. I must also avoid procrastination and refrain from putting rattlesnakes under my bed by lying or doing things I must keep hidden. God will give me the magic of a calm spirit, but my behavior must prepare and maintain the channel of God's
grace.

I love you all.

October 5

Good morning.

Our keynote is "Humility".

The Meditation for the Day stresses the good which flows from tolerance, sympathy and understanding of others. If I choose that angle of approach, I will behave exactly as if I were seeking to love, comfort and understand others. The same behavior will ensue if I follow the AA Code of, "Love and tolerance of others".

Behavior consistent with the Biblical Golden Rule will also be identical.

It is the same eternal message of Love. That message comes to us from so many spiritual sources and in so many different voices that its universal truth and importance is undeniable.

Acting out Love is the source of usefulness, peace, harmony with God and charmed relationships with my fellows. When living in Love, I am living in God's Magic.

When we behave lovingly I believe we begin to bear a slight resemblance to our Creator. In the end, Love may be all there is.

I love you all.

October 6

Good morning.

The keynote is "Honesty."

Today's meditation and prayer discuss positive personal change. I have squandered much of my lifetime vainly trying to change myself with my own resources. Behaving like a person with some humility and acceptance of their powerlessness proved to be my key to positive change. It turns out that real change in me comes from God, but begins with my surrender.

I must accept that I cannot change the way I am, and even further, that I don't even know who or what I should be. A farmer doesn't grow things, but creates an environment in which growth will take place, and God grows things. Doctors don't heal. They take action to facilitate healing, and God heals.

When I give up on engineering changes in my being and humbly concentrate on taking the next stitch as the Divine Spark directs, God's magic takes over.

By taking one Divinely guided stitch at a time, I create a situation in which God will change me. Then God begins to move me toward who and what I should be, as I take one right stitch at a time.

I love you all.

October 7

Good morning.

Our keynote is "Humbly say to ourselves many times today, 'Thy will be done.'"

The Thought for the Day is a reminder that even the best of us are imperfect. Few defects are more crippling than a demand for perfection in myself or my fellows. That impossible expectation of myself results in procrastination, paralysis, endless self-recrimination, and often, failure. It robs me of the ability to focus on simply the next stitch.

Requiring perfection in others tragically impacts my relationships by assuring disappointment and inviting bitterness and loneliness. It can blind me to truth because all our messengers are imperfect. If we could only receive valid messages from perfect human messengers, none of us would ever receive a single valid message.

Peace, success, and enlightenment seem to come not so much from human strength (my own or others') as from loving acceptance of all our weaknesses. Accepting human weakness allows the inflow of God's strength and Magic.

I love you all.

October 8

Good morning.

Our keynote is "Pray to seek to love, comfort, and understand..."

The Prayer for the Day asks that I may strive for true tolerance and understanding of my fellows. In pursuit of that goal, keeping thoughts of God and others foremost in mind is both the key and my greatest challenge. Thinking about myself is easy. It is my default position. In seeking to be truly tolerant and understanding, I must strive to let God overcome my self-centered nature, one stitch at a time.

Seeking to be courteous in every single human encounter is a huge step toward tolerance and understanding. I believe courtesy is the most underrated of all spiritual traits. It is impossible for me to be discourteous and spiritual simultaneously. Silently and repetitively praying to love, comfort, and understand is my most effective tool for shifting my focus to God and others.

If I am persistently courteous and repetitively pray to love, comfort, and understand, God magically moves me toward tolerance and understanding.

I love you all.

October 9

Good morning.

Our keynote is "Help God's kids do what they need to have done."

The Thought for the Day warns that we will sometimes find our fellows intrusive, dull, repetitive, and irritating. When my initial reaction to someone is negative and I just want to get rid of them, I need to pause, say a prayer, and bring to mind the AA Code of "Love and tolerance of others." One approach to "tolerating" someone whom I find unpleasant is to paste an interested look on my face and try not to fidget while I endure and plot my escape. I can get through the encounter that way, but there will be little value or joy for either party.

The far superior approach is to love. If I will pray to love, comfort, and understand and give my entire interest, attention, and love to the "offensive" person, magic happens. I become a listener, and my impatience and irritation evaporate. For that moment, the other child of God becomes the most interesting thing in the world. Love has transformed the encounter, and often, a mutually rewarding friendship has begun.

I love you all.

October 10

Good morning.

Our keynote is "Persistence."

The Thought, Meditation, and Prayer for the Day all touch on serving others and God, regardless of our own discomfort and inconvenience.

When I am secure in my faith, enjoy the people involved, feel good physically, have plenty of time, and am not obsessed with my own problems, it is easy to love and give.

However, it is when those things are not going as I want that serving God and others is most critical and most rewarding.

Giving only what I feel like giving, when I want to give it, to people I want to help, is not really serving God or others. It is serving myself.

The magic happens when I try to give what I don't feel like giving and don't have time to give to those I don't particularly enjoy serving. Once I begin to give, despite not feeling I have anything to give or wanting to do so, the Spirit flows in, and I begin to feel lovingly toward and enjoy serving the very people I had wanted to avoid.

And then, I have truly given and have served others and God.

I love you all.

October 11

Good morning.

Our keynote is "Courtesy."

Today's Meditation and Prayer emphasize harmony with our fellows as necessary if we are to experience the magic of harmony with God.

I find courtesy to be the threshold of harmony with, and love for, my fellows. Also, I have come to believe that it is impossible for me to be spiritual or in harmony with God while being discourteous.

Courtesy, in my experience, is the most underrated of all spiritual principles. It opens the door to harmony.

Seeking to love, comfort, and understand, rather than to be loved, comforted, and understood, brings that harmony into reality.

So, my seemingly insignificant courtesy to the next person I encounter is actually a first step toward harmony with humankind, God, and myself.

Seeking to be unfailingly courteous has a magical effect on my life and the people around me.

I love you all.

October 12

Good morning.

Our keynote is "Gratitude."

Today's Meditation stresses the importance of doing the little things in service of God and others.

My ego's attraction to "big deals" makes me think of serving God and others in the manner of Mother Theresa, Bill W., Chuck C., etc. When I, and my opportunities to be helpful, fall so woefully short of those giants, there is a tendency to feel, "What's the use anyway?"

I am reminded of a wonderful story about an impoverished widow who quietly gave much of the little she had. It turned out that her gift was far greater than the obscenely large amount conspicuously given by a rich man.

The magic is in persistently performing small, quiet kindnesses, not in big splashy public displays.

I love you all.

October 13

Good morning.

Our keynote is "Humility."

The Meditation for the Day urges us to keep progressing in the spiritual life and cautions us, "Do not misspend time over past failures."

That brings to mind Cherry's oft-repeated belief that self-recrimination is the single most useless and counterproductive of all human endeavors.

While it may feel somehow noble to weep and wail over past errors, there is nothing useful or noble about it. It merely compounds the original error and impedes me in making amends.

A few years ago, I stopped praying for God to forgive me and allow me to forgive myself. Instead, I began thanking God for having forgiven me and for having allowed me to forgive myself. That simple change in my prayers has diminished the burden of my past behavior.

It helps me avoid repeating mistakes and has made me more effective in setting right the damage I have caused. It has worked like magic!

I love you all.

October 14

Good morning.

Our keynote is "Honesty."

Today's Meditation and Prayer continue encouraging us not to dwell on and be limited by previous failures and mistakes.

There is a persistent voice in me which insists that I have put myself beyond forgiveness or hope.

It is ever-present, whether its subject is my life as a whole or some relatively trivial current endeavor.

It wants me to believe I have strayed so far from God's will that there is no longer a next right action.

That voice is a lethal liar. It is darkness trying to reclaim me.

Refusal to forgive myself is not noble; it is the rejection of God's forgiveness.

My experience is that the truly unforgivable sin is the refusal to behave as one who has forgiven oneself.

I have found God to be all-forgiving. It is my ego that insists upon miring me in the failures and mistakes of five seconds or fifty years ago.

I find The Magic by accepting forgiveness and beginning anew in the right now.

I love you all.

October 15

Good morning.

Our keynote is: "Humbly say to ourselves many times today, 'Thy will be done...'"

The Meditation for the Day declares living in accordance with God's will to be the only path to a fully satisfying life.

Behaving as directed by the Divine Spark, one stitch at a time, is the only way I know to live as God would have me live.

If I am disturbed by a situation (e.g., that my bed is unmade), but I don't feel like doing what I need to do, I can choose either of two courses.

1. I can pray for God to change my mind and feelings, so I will want to make the bed, call my AA sponsor about "the issue," write an inventory on it, and eventually get some outside counseling on the matter.

If I choose that route, I will never find peace or satisfaction. The unmade bed will take over my life.

Or,

2. I can thank God for the strength to accomplish the task, despite not wanting to do so, and immediately get busy making the bed.

The second choice is my only route back to peace and The Magic.

God won't, and human help can't, give me peace if I don't do what I need to do.

I love you all.

October 16

Good morning.

Our keynote is: "Pray to seek to love, comfort, and understand..."

The Meditation and Prayer for the Day tell us that improving our inner selves by our behavior will change our outward circumstances for the better. My experience in sobriety verifies that claim.

When my primary objective is improving my material circumstances, I am more likely to get the snakepit than improved circumstances.

But when my first priority is to help God's kids and take the next stitch as the Divine Spark directs, my worldly circumstances fall into place beautifully.

AA's Big Book says material well-being always follows spiritual growth; it is never the other way around.

My mind and ego don't understand how that happens, but experience convinces me that God's Magic World works exactly so.

I love you all.

October 17

Good morning.

Our keynote is: "Help God's kids do what they need to have done."

Today's Meditation and Prayer emphasize how much better our lives will be if we focus on God and others rather than ourselves.

Socrates said, "The unexamined life is not worth living."

While I agree, he could have added that the obsessively over-examined life is even worse.

I love the story of the centipede who started thinking about the individual movements of its 100 legs. As the fable goes, the centipede became so confused by its self-obsession that it finally was unable to move at all.

So it is with me.

Excessive self-consciousness robs me of peace and effectiveness. I am most useful, effective, and happy when I am thinking of God and other people and thinking of me only in terms of God's will for my next action.

When I am lost in the morass of self, I can find neither my way nor The Magic.

I love you all.

October 18

Good morning.

Our keynote is "Persistence."

Humility, the most critical and elusive of all spiritual attributes, is the subject of today's Meditation and Prayer.

My very first step toward humility is maintaining consciousness of God and of my own limited understanding and power.

Being mindful that the only glimpse of God's will I ever get is in the instant, and only for my next action, gives me a realistic view of my capacity to understand.

Remaining aware that the only power I ever have is over my own next action discourages me from "big dealism."

Acceptance of those limitations opens the door for humility.

It also helps to remain aware that I did nothing to deserve the gift of being a sober, living magical creature in God's Magic World today. I have no right to any of this.

It is all God's grace.

It is further humbling to remember that my thoughts, feelings, and beliefs, which seem like the center of the universe to me, are of little interest to the other 7 billion people on the planet.

If I strive to keep those things in mind and behave accordingly, MAYBE, once in a while, without my awareness, I will be gifted with a tiny bit of true humility.

I love you all.

October 19

Good morning.

Our keynote is "Courtesy".

Today's Prayer asks that we may trust God's responses to our prayers, regardless of whether they seem to be what we had in mind.

It invites reflection on the countless times I would have cheated myself if God had answered my prayers in the form I envisioned.

It also brings to mind the difference between faith and hope. I have wasted a lot of time trying to have faith that God will arrange things in specific ways so I will be okay.

I now know that such prayers are based on hope, not faith. They actually are self-will dressed in spiritual clothing.

I am not dealing with faith until I am seeking to know that all will be well, regardless of specific results in human matters.

If I persist in stitching as the Divine Spark guides, I will be led to the magic of God's perfect results, despite my inability to see that I am moving in that direction.

For me, the essence of faith is taking the next right action when my limited brain can't see that it leads to where I should be.

I love you all.

October 20

Good morning.

Our keynote is "Gratitude".

Today's Meditation and Prayer urge us to be aware of and content with the working out of God's will in our lives.

There is an old story that beautifully illustrates my blind and stubborn refusal to acknowledge the hand of God during my drinking years.

An atheist was telling a believer that he knew there was no God because he had been the sole survivor of a plane crash in the Arctic. After hours of wandering hopelessly in the frozen wilderness, he finally, in desperation, prayed for God to save him. According to the atheist, God did nothing.

The confused believer said, "But obviously you survived."

The atheist replied, "Yes, but God had nothing to do with it. About five minutes after I prayed, an Eskimo came along."

Today, I pray to see God's Magic behind all the "Eskimos" who are sent for me.

I love you all.

October 21

Good morning.

Our keynote is "Humility".

The Meditation for the Day tells us that God knocks gently at the door of the human heart and that The Divine's availability to us is not based upon our merit or lack of it.

God's knocking is indeed gentle and perilously easy to ignore.

In my experience, I don't open my heart's door to God just once and then it remains open. I often have to either answer the door or ignore the soft Divine tapping many times in the course of a single day.

Regardless of how many times I ignore the knocking, God is always there, IF I will open the door.

My first sponsor, Cherry, said there is nothing we can do to make God love us less or more. Divine love is constant, but if I am to live in God's Magic, I must persistently answer the Divine knocking.

Cherry added that God is courteous and doesn't intrude if unwanted. Therefore, waiting for God to kick in the door will likely be in vain.

I love you all.

October 22

Good morning.

Our keynote is "Honesty".

Today's Meditation and Prayer speak of building an unshakable faith through the persistent renewal of faith.

Experience has taught me that faith is not a state of mind that, once attained, will endure forever. My faith is only as strong as my persistence in behaving faithfully.

I cannot immediately control my spiritual, mental, or emotional state. However, God gives me absolute control over my own next action.

If I persist in taking those next actions in accordance with faith, my fear and doubt will be overcome. I will feel secure in God's hands and will return to the heart of God's Magic.

Despite the fluctuations in my thoughts, feelings, and beliefs, my faith will remain unshakable as long as my persistence in faithful action is unshakable.

I love you all.

October 23

Good morning.

Our keynote is "Humbly say to ourselves many times today, 'Thy will be done'...".

The Meditation for the Day states a powerful cautionary truth about interactions with our fellow human beings: "Between one human being and another, only spiritual forces will suffice to keep them in harmony."

I often express the same idea by saying that human relations are ultimately humanly impossible.

My most effective approach for bringing spirituality into human interaction is fourfold:

1. Always be courteous.
2. Seek to give each person my entire interest, attention, and love.
3. Pray to love, comfort, and understand before and during encounters.
4. Never give unsolicited advice or otherwise criticize.

This approach works with the people closest to me, in fleeting encounters with strangers, and everywhere in between. It has a magical effect on my interactions with all people.

I love you all.

October 24

Good morning.

Our keynote is "Pray to seek to love, comfort and understand...".

The beautiful Thought for the Day is about the relief that comes from humbly accepting my limitations. It is a roadmap to relief from the bondage of self: relief from trying to wrest my needs from the unwilling grasp of a hostile universe, relief from being the ant trying to steer a log that is floating down the river, relief from the impossible task of trying to manipulate others into loving, comforting, and understanding me, relief from being at the center of a universe that is all about me, and relief from being enslaved by my own thoughts, feelings, and beliefs.

All that blessed relief flows from simply accepting the limitations of my understanding and power, maintaining consciousness of God, and behaving one stitch at a time as directed by the Divine Spark. If I keep it that simple, magically, the whole power of the universe supports me instead of frustrating me.

I love you all.

October 25

Good morning.

Our keynote is "Help God's kids do what they need to have done."

Today's Meditation acknowledges that we can never completely overcome our selfishness. There is relief and freedom in that realization, as long as I don't use it as an excuse to behave selfishly.

While I will never be free of selfish thoughts and desires, I don't have to let them dictate my actions. If I persistently seek to behave unselfishly, one stitch at a time, and maintain God consciousness, something magical happens; with each little unselfish stitch, the bondage of self loosens.

Today I gauge my level of selfishness by my behavior, not by what I want to do or what I think, feel, or believe. Only my actions ever leave a footprint on reality.

Today I pray that my behavior will not be enslaved to the crazy, selfish picture show in my head, but will be guided by the Divine Spark in my heart.

I love you all.

October 26

Good morning.

Our keynote is "Courtesy".

The Meditation for the Day focuses on the battle fought within each of us between the material and spiritual approaches to life.

In my own experience, there has never been a single epic battle resolving once and for all whether I will walk the spiritual path or the material. Instead, each day brings a number of small skirmishes with mixed outcomes.

Successfully living the spiritual life doesn't happen by simply forming an intention to do so. It is critical for me to realize that my intentions are not decisions, and I must be careful not to view them as such. Merely forming an intention to walk the spiritual path only becomes a decision if I take persistent action on it, one stitch at a time.

If I am to know the magic of the spiritual life, it will not be through my mind; it will be the result of persistent spiritual behavior. As the AA Big Book says, "The spiritual life is not a theory. We have to live it."

I love you all.

October 27

Good morning.

Our keynote is "Persistence".

Our reading today tells us, "Walk all the way with another person and with God. Do not go part of the way and then stop."

I need to keep that principle in mind every day. I have always been a flashy sprinter but have trouble continuing after the new has worn off or something is no longer convenient.

I suspect there is little spiritual value in helping people only when it is convenient and I want to do it.

Today, I pray that I will persist in seeking to do God's will, one stitch at a time, and trying to help God's kids, especially when I don't feel like doing either.

Perfection is not on the menu for me. I owe my sobriety and life to persistence and am convinced it is one of the most underrated and under-discussed spiritual principles.

It is by persisting when I am tired, doubtful, fearful, and want to quit that I find God's Magic, harmony with my fellows, and success.

I love you all.

October 28

Good morning.

Our keynote is "Humility".

The Prayer for the Day asks that I may accept my inability to see God's will beyond my own very next stitch (i.e., action). It goes on to ask that I may be content with God's guidance for only that single stitch.

Acceptance of the truth underlying that prayer has proved to be essential if I am to live a successful life of usefulness, peace, spirituality, and effectiveness.

Like most of us, I have wasted much of my life chasing the myth of human security by trying to see the future.

In the end, that quest has always left me empty and afraid.

On the other hand, if I relinquish my futile demand to know and control the future, things change.

I can then focus only on my next action as directed by the part of God within each of us, which I call the Divine Spark.

The results flowing from that angle of approach are magical.

I am then filled with peace, faith, and hope. I walk with God into the future unafraid.

God indeed lights my path but with a penlight for a single step; never a floodlight revealing more of the path.

I love you all.

October 29

Good morning.

Our keynote is "Gratitude".

Today's Meditation and Prayer urge us to behave in such a way that our lives will be a demonstration of the power of God, recovery, and spirituality.

The Big Book describes that demonstration as "carrying the message".

It has long been my belief that courtesy is the most underrated of all spiritual traits. I believe it facilitates "carrying the message" more than any other attribute.

When we are courteous, people see love and peace in us. They are much more open to the message we carry.

I believe it is impossible to be discourteous and spiritual at the same moment.

By simply being courteous, we make significant progress towards seeking to love, comfort, and understand our fellows.

Sadly, we often find it easier to be courteous to strangers than to those closest to us. Every little discourtesy to our loved ones leaves a scar.

Today, I pray to be unfailingly courteous to every person I encounter.

Courtesy really is magic in human relations.

It is love.

I love you all.

October 30

Good morning.

Our keynote is "Humility".

Today's reading is about waiting patiently for things to happen in God's time. When I am scared and stressed, my mind screams, "Do something, even if it's wrong!" My first sponsor, Cherry, repeatedly called that approach the single craziest premise on which he ran his life prior to sobriety. Until the Divine Spark's guidance becomes clear, he taught it is more prudent to do nothing than engage in blind, frantic activity.

I have robbed myself many times by rashly causing the "other shoe" to prematurely drop. Just as I am handsomely rewarded for my patience, I am severely penalized by my childish lack of it. In my extreme impatience, I sometimes consciously and insanely cause the worst possible outcome rather than endure more waiting.

I was also taught that God doesn't withhold anything from us once we have grown spiritually able to have it without hurting ourselves or someone else. The magic is in waiting for God's time. It is never in my frantic, impatient self-will.

I love you all.

October 31

Good morning.

Our keynote is "Honesty".

Today's Meditation and Prayer describe how we are miraculously transformed by becoming aware of and embracing the part of God which is deep down inside each of us. It does indeed "change our whole attitude toward life". I call the God within us the Spark of the Divine.

When thinking of God and following the guidance of the Divine Spark, I am much more likely to be sober, grateful, humble, honest, courteous, effective, and useful to my fellows and God. The alternative to thinking about and being guided by God is to think about and take orders from myself. That angle of approach strips me of all the above benefits and ultimately leads to the abyss.

Emmett Fox wrote in the Golden Key that thinking of God will make any difficulty go away. From experience, I can add that excessively thinking about any difficulty and myself will cause the difficulty to grow and will open the door for a legion of other difficulties.

Persistently thinking of God is my first step toward living in awareness of the Magic.

I love you all.

NOVEMBER

November 1

Good morning.

Our keynote is "Humbly say to ourselves many times today, 'Thy will be done'..."

Today's reading discusses faith and hope.

In early sobriety, I had the two confused for a long time. If I fail to take the daily action necessary to maintain my spiritual condition, I will still confuse them today.

I've wasted a lot of time trying to have faith that my health, relationships, finances, loved ones, etc. will be okay in human terms.

I now know that attempting to have faith that God will cause human events and conditions to be as I wish is futile. My desires for human results are not subject to faith. They are hope and, largely, self-will.

I am in quest of faith only if I seek to know that all will be well, regardless of how disastrous earthly events appear.

In our limited perception, the ultimate future of any human being does not look attractive.

Thus, my prayer today is to have faith that, even when the inevitable apparent human tragedies I fear actually happen, I will remain safe and protected in God's loving hands.

When the magic of real faith surrounds me, God has put me beyond fear of human tragedy and freed me from hoping human events take historically impossible turns. I am protected by the magic merger of acceptance and faith.

I love you all.

November 2

Our keynote is: "Pray to seek to love, comfort and understand..."

Today's reading emphasizes the futility of trying to hoard blessings to ourselves.

In my experience, that futility encompasses both spiritual and material blessings.

AA members must continually pass on their own good fortune in order to maintain and enjoy their sobriety. Other attempts to live a spiritual life without sharing it often seem to result in a withered spirit.

In the material world we see people hoard wealth to themselves and sometimes that wealth continues to grow. I don't believe that invalidates the principle. In my observation, such people lose the ability to take joy in their material well-being.

So, ultimately, even as net worth skyrockets, its value to the miser diminishes.

I find The Magic in realizing that it truly is by giving that we receive.

I love you all.

November 3

Good morning.

Our keynote is: "Help God's kids do what they need to have done."

Charity, today's reading explains, is another word for love.

The Thought for the Day defines love, or charity, as an unselfish, outgoing desire to help other people.

For my purposes, I amend that definition to, "BEHAVING as one who has an unselfish, outgoing desire to help other people."

For half my life I was absolutely certain that whether or not I loved was determined by how I felt. For many years now, I have been equally convinced that I am only as loving as I behave, and that the value of my loving actions is neither enhanced nor diminished by my thoughts, feelings, or beliefs.

Action is love and love is action.

To claim to love and not behave lovingly is empty hypocrisy.

On the other hand, the power of loving behavior is not diminished by the occasional waning of our loving feelings.

Part of The Magic is that the more lovingly I behave, the more feelings of love I will enjoy.

I love you all.

November 4

Good morning.

Our keynote is "Persistence".

Today's Meditation and Prayer tell us that happiness cannot be attained by directly seeking it. If we are to find happiness and know the fulfillment of joy, it will be as a byproduct of right living.

My experience has validated that truth over and over. That I still must regularly rediscover it exposes my inability to completely refrain from trying to live for myself.

Selfish and self-centered motives are so ingrained that I will never, in this life, be completely free of them.

Despite my serial failures, persistently starting over in trying to lay aside self and take the next stitch as directed has brought much progress and happiness. Persistent positive behavior following failure leads me to the perfect Magic, despite my own imperfection.

The cycle of persistence, failure, and more persistence is the only spiritual growth of which I am capable.

My loving God seems to smile on my persistence and forgive my errant stitches.

I love you all.

November 5

Good morning.

Our keynote is "Courtesy".

The Thought for the Day describes the crippling effects of fear and the value of faith in our daily struggles with that fear.

It is as if I have an inner "faith/fear container." It can only hold so much of either or both. To the extent I have one, I cannot have the other.

Prior to sobriety, I had no faith, so I was full of fear.

My most effective course to replace fear with faith has been threefold:

1. Praying, not so much for the removal of fear as for the strength to act in the face of it.
2. Concentrating on seeking to love, comfort, and understand others rather than on whether I am loved, comforted, and understood. I am rarely afraid unless I am thinking about me.
3. Using Emmet Fox's Golden Key to help me think of God rather than the source of my fear. As Emmet promises, when I succeed in thinking of God rather than that which I fear, the fear evaporates.

The Magic is in thinking of God and others. Terror and the abyss lie in thinking only of myself.

I love you all.

November 6

Good morning.

Our keynote is "Gratitude".

The Thought for the Day continues the discussion of fear.

My excursions into the past and/or the future (on which God never accompanies me!) are where I encounter most of my fears. If I stay in the moment, with God, I am armored against fear's destruction of peace, usefulness, and effectiveness.

It has been helpful through the years to remember that F-E-A-R is an acronym for "False Events Appearing Real". Likewise, I have often been heartened by Mark Twain's quip: "My life has been filled with many tragedies; almost none of which ever happened".

If I keep those things in mind and take to heart Cherry's warning that self-recrimination is the most useless and counterproductive of all human endeavors, I am protected. Yesterday's and tomorrow's fears won't devour today.

God's Magic is ONLY in the right now.

I love you all.

November 7

Good morning.

Our keynote is "Humility".

The Meditation for the Day reminds us that it is God's Magic, power, and grace flowing through us, not ourselves, which helps those around us.

If I use my intellect alone in seeking to address other people's problems, I am nothing but an unqualified and ineffective counselor. Also, I am usually talking with people who have a condition which does not respond well to even qualified psychological counseling.

When asked for guidance, I first need to lay aside any notion that I must (or can) articulate answers or solutions from my own wits. Next, I need to pray to give the person and their circumstances my entire interest, attention, and love.

Then, if I silently repeat a prayer to love, comfort, understand and to speak the quiet, loving truth, God may work through me.

I pray today to remember that I have no magic, power, or grace. At best, I can only be a channel for God's Magic, power, and grace.

I love you all.

November 8

Good morning.

Our keynote is "Honesty".

Today's Meditation and Prayer caution us that dwelling on the past will impair or destroy our usefulness and peace.

It was repeatedly impressed on me in early sobriety that self-recrimination is the most useless and counterproductive of all human endeavors.

However, mere awareness that morbid reflection will poison my life does not free me from it. I must take action.

The threshold of freedom from the past was making amends to all persons I had harmed through AA's Steps eight and nine. Once my amends were completed, I experienced much relief and freedom.

However, I quickly discovered that my emancipation would be short-lived unless, going forward, I persistently kept it clean by promptly admitting and setting right any new mistakes as directed by Step ten.

Prayer, thinking of others, being honest and open, and maintaining God consciousness allow me to stay in The Magic of right now with God.

Finally, I must keep in mind that the past is the past. Regardless of whether it was fifty years or five seconds ago, the same rules apply.

I love you all.

November 9

Good morning.

Our keynote is: "Humbly say to ourselves many times today, 'Thy will be done'..."

The Thought for the Day urges us to be less negative and more positive.

In early sobriety, I was frequently told that I needed a more positive attitude. I believed my attitude to be my thoughts, feelings, and beliefs, and set about trying to change them. I prayed, read inspirational literature, did step work, etc., but made no real progress.

One day, I was given a new definition of "attitude," which has nothing to do with my thoughts, feelings, or beliefs. It is, "angle of approach".

My life changed on the spot and has remained so for 41 years. It is one of my greatest epiphanies.

My "angle of approach" is how I behave toward a person or situation, not what I think, feel, or believe.

God gives me no immediate power over my thoughts, feelings, or beliefs, but does give me dominion over my own next action.

My new definition instantly transformed my "attitude" from beyond my control to absolutely within my control.

My behavior changes my thoughts, feelings, and beliefs. It is never the other way around.

When behaving as a magical creature living in God's Magic World, I get to be exactly that regardless of the old crazy picture show in my head!

I love you all.

November 10

Good morning.

Our keynote is: "Pray to seek to love, comfort, and understand..."

The Meditation and Prayer for the Day urge us not to be overwhelmed or paralyzed by trouble, difficulties, or failure.

More than 30 years ago, I met a long-time dry alcoholic who, for many years, had been living underground in Las Vegas and successfully playing poker for a living. Having known a few people who failed spectacularly at that endeavor, I asked how he was able to succeed.

He replied that his success had nothing to do with the good hands; anyone can win playing them. At the end of the day, he continued, the entire difference between success and failure is what is done with the worst hands one is dealt.

I have found that message to be priceless and applicable to every area of my life. The mountaintops of success are delightful, but The Magic is in what I do in the valleys of failure and despair.

I pray today to give my entire interest, attention, and love to the very worst "hands" God deals me in every aspect of my life.

I love you all.

November 11

Good morning.

Our keynote is: "Help God's kids do what they need to have done..."

The Thought for the Day asks, "Do I realize that I am not so important after all?".

Remaining aware of my unimportance is critical if I am to be useful, effective, and at peace. Yet, my default position is to let myself and how I feel be the most important thing in the world to me.

If I fail to take the action necessary to maintain my spiritual condition today, I will revert to that default position.

I pray to keep in mind that my thoughts, feelings, and beliefs are of little interest to the world or (I believe) to God. I am judged wholly on my behavior.

If my behavior is directed toward seeking to be loved, comforted, and understood, I have put my ego and my feelings back in charge and am on a fast track to the snake pit.

It is acting out of concern for my fellows and maintaining consciousness of God which renders the crazy picture show in my head powerless and frees me from the bondage of self.

The Magic materializes when my angle of approach is, "Big God, big you, and little me."

I love you all.

November 12

Good morning.

Our keynote is "Persistence".

The Thought for the Day asks if I have become less critical of people.

I surely hope so.

Many years ago, I scoured the Big Book looking for directions on how to tell people what is wrong with them. I found none.

I suspect there are no directions because I simply don't need to correct people unless it is part of my job description.

Of course, occasionally, it seems clearly God's will for me to set someone aright. It has never worked out well one single time in my life.

As Cherry said, if God wanted me to be a policeman, I could tell because I would have a badge and a gun. If God wanted me to be a judge, I would have a robe and a gavel.

Having none of those things, I am well-advised to refrain from policing or judging.

I need to be courteous to all and remember that unsolicited advice is always criticism.

No exceptions!

The Magic is in building up my fellows, not tearing them down.

Today, I pray to seek to make the day a little brighter for everyone I encounter and to never unnecessarily make it darker.

I love you all.

November 13

Good morning.

Our keynote is "Gratitude".

The Thought for the Day asks, "Am I less harsh in my judgment of people?"

For the first few years of my sobriety, I was greatly troubled by what I believed to be my near constant judgment of others. My mind involuntarily formed judgments (generally negative) of most people I even glimpsed. I prayed, discussed it with sponsors, and did inventories, but the old crazy picture show in my head continued to roll.

Then, my prayers began to be answered in an unexpected way. I realized that those unwelcome judgmental thoughts are beyond my control and, like all my thoughts, feelings, and beliefs, have absolutely no impact on reality. Like my attitude, whether I am judgmental is determined not by involuntary, fleeting thoughts and feelings, but by my actions.

Serial baseless judgmental thoughts still fly through my head, but they no longer bother me. In fact, I often chuckle at them. I have known for years that I am not judgmental unless I behave judgmentally. God and the world do not judge me on thoughts and feelings, which I cannot control, but rather on actions, which I can control. The action is The Magic.

I love you all.

November 14

Good morning.

Our keynote is "Gratitude".

The Thought for the Day continues the discussion of judgment and criticism. It suggests pushing past initial negative impressions to relentlessly look for the good in everyone. Adopting that angle of approach has magically transformed my world.

My life is filled with dear friends and treasured and admired fellow travelers who were initially judged, criticized, and dismissed by the old crazy picture show in my head.

When I ignore my rash and harsh first impression of someone and pray to seek to love, comfort, and understand him or her, miracles happen. As I seek to give them my entire interest, attention, and love, the dull become fascinating. The snobbish become sophisticated and warm. The obnoxious become invigorating and amusing. The ignorant acquire a precious simple wisdom.

I truly do have a magic, magnifying mind. That on which I focus grows and that which I ignore fades away.

I love you all.

November 15

Good morning.

Our keynote is "Humility".

The Thought for the Day asks if we have made progress with our tendency to self-pity and "sensitivity".

If I am on the alert for slights and failures to respect me, I will find them in abundance. It is inevitable because when looking for such things, I am seeking to be loved, comforted, and understood.

I have found it to be an absolute spiritual law that if I am seeking love, comfort, and understanding, I will not find it to my satisfaction. The only time it is possible for me to feel adequately loved, comforted, and understood is when I persistently pray and seek to love, comfort, and understand others, rather than seeking the same for myself.

Many years ago, a fellow opined in an AA meeting that alcoholics just seem to have more pain than other people. My dear, late friend and sponsor, Bernie, boomed out, "Bulls**t! We are just bigger cry babies!".

My "sensitivity" is just another form of self-obsession that blocks me from The Magic.

I love you all.

November 16

Good morning.

Our keynote is "Honesty".

The Thought for the Day asks if I am refraining from doing things (or failing to do things) which cause inner conflict, guilt, fear, and self-loathing.

One of the greatest turning points in my life came when Cherry explained the only key to a comfortable life. He said prayer, meditation, meetings, and 12-step work are absolutely necessary. However, he continued, those things will not overcome my own behavior.

He put it very simply. The ONLY way to be comfortable in the long run is to do things (however immediately uncomfortable they may be) that will eventually make me comfortable and not do things (however immediately attractive they are) that will eventually yield discomfort.

Since that day, part of my morning meditation has been making a list of things to do that day. They are things which, if done, will result in comfort and, if undone, will result in discomfort.

Listing those things and doing them has magically changed my life.

I love you all.

November 17

Good morning.

Our keynote is: "Humbly say to ourselves many times each day, 'Thy will be done'..."

The Prayer for the Day asks that I may neither desire the world's applause nor seek rewards for doing what I believe is right.

Seeking applause or rewards is just a form of demanding love, comfort, and understanding.

Mark Twain's observation comes to mind: "I have been complimented many times and it always makes me uncomfortable; I never feel they have said enough."

It's a spiritual law that if I am seeking applause and rewards, I will never find them in sufficient quantity.

Also, I firmly believe that doing the right thing for the wrong reason is far better than not doing it at all. However, if it is all contrived for my selfish ends, it is not likely to ring true or produce the desired results or rewards.

The Magic is in doing right simply because it is right.

I love you all.

November 18

Good morning.

Our keynote is: "Help God's kids do what they need to have done..."

The Thought for the Day discusses procrastination, which is simply sloth. That deadly sin has caused me more pain and fear than even alcohol and other drugs.

I suspect my procrastination is fueled by egotistical and ridiculous perfectionism, fear of looking bad, and a generous dollop of plain old laziness.

However, contrary to our society's pervasive myth, figuring out why I have a character defect doesn't make it go away.

My only progress comes when I add action to my prayers.

I have read, prayed, talked with sponsors, done inventories, and sought outside counseling to try to overcome my procrastination. None of it accomplished much.

Changing my prayers from asking God to remove my fear to thanking God for giving me the strength to act in spite of my fear has yielded much growth.

The motto, "Better 'done' than 'perfect'", has also worked magic on my procrastination.

I love you all.

November 19

Good morning.

Our keynote is "Pray to seek to love, comfort, and understand..."

Today's meditation and prayer encourage us to maintain consciousness of God by focusing on goodness and beauty.

My daily reference to "The Magic" reminds me to choose that very angle of approach and cherish the priceless gift of a day as a living, sober human being.

When I consider all the millions of days which came before I was alive, and will come after I am gone from this world, the mathematical odds against me being part of The Magic on this specific day are greater than the odds against winning Powerball. Each day of human life is a greater, less likely gift than winning the lottery.

I pray to never again squander the gift of being a magical creature in God's Magic World. Too many times I have thrown the gift back in God's face because I didn't like the way it was wrapped.

I love you all.

November 20

Good morning.

Our keynote is "Persistence."

"There is a weariness in an abundance of things," declares the meditation for the day.

I have a great deal of experience with that particular weariness.

Cherry taught me that material things are spiritually neutral. It is my angle of approach which turns them into either a blessing or a burden.

On days when I view my family, law practice, money, house, car, reputation, etc. to be MINE, I wind up empty, exhausted, and in chaos trying to manage and protect them.

On days when I view them all as belonging to God and am grateful for the gift of having them in my life for the day, they become a joy and tools for being helpful, rather than a spiritual impediment.

The Magic is in having only undeserved gifts from a loving God and nothing which I have wrested from the unwilling grip of a hostile universe by my efforts and guile.

Lord knows, I'm grateful I didn't get what I deserved but instead, mercy from a loving God.

I love you all.

November 21

Good morning.

Our keynote is "Courtesy."

The prayer for the day asks that I may be more comfortable in my way of living and feel more at home and at peace with myself.

It is a beautiful prayer with lofty goals. However, merely praying has never transported me to that sublime state. My many visits to a place of true peace and comfort with myself have always resulted from a partnership with God.

When I pray and then persistently seek to do God's will, one stitch at a time, The Magic comes to visit.

If I look to the things of this world for peace, comfort, and security, I will not find them. Worldly things and pursuits can only give me a fleeting illusion of peace, comfort, and security.

It is God's grace, coupled with my faithful stitching, which brings The Magic.

I love you all.

November 22

Good morning.

Our keynote is "Gratitude."

The Thought, Meditation, and Prayer for the Day all discuss boredom, self-centeredness, and love.

Long ago, I was told that believing I am or trying to be interesting ensures that people will not find me interesting. The surest way to bore others is to think and talk mainly about myself. Additionally, I am initially bored stiff by another person's self-centered chatter. It can require a lot of silent prayer to become interested in self-centered chatter, but it can be done.

My solution to boredom, as well as being boring, is seeking to give my entire interest, attention, and love to others. Magically, however dull someone initially seems, really listening to and seeking to love, comfort, and understand them makes them interesting to me. It works the other way around too. No one seems to find me boring when I seek to give them my entire interest, attention, and love! Loving action directed toward others is my universal antidote to boredom.

I love you all.

November 23

Good morning.

Our keynote is "Humility."

Today's reading warns us against being paralyzed by fear of failure or even actual failure.

There is a lethal voice in me which repeatedly tells me I am incapable of doing what needs to be done or have already failed so miserably that there is no longer an effective next right action. It is the voice of doom and hopelessness. If I submit to it, I am truly lost.

Most successful endeavors, in all areas of my life, have flowed from doing things the voice was telling me I could not do. Usually, in the course of ultimately succeeding, I have failed, and the voice has screamed, "All is lost; no use to go on". Experience has taught me that God doesn't put things in my path without giving me the strength and tools to deal with them and that I can't stray so far from God's will that there is no longer a next right action. So many times, The Magic has come from acting in the face of fear and hopelessness. Persistence is all!

I love you all.

November 24

Good morning.

Our keynote is "Honesty."

The Thought for the Day tells us that no AA member has ever "arrived."

I believe the same is true of all spiritual seekers.

I spent years clinging to the myth that when the present storm passed, the object of my obsession was obtained, the epiphany was realized, or the anticipated positive event happened, I would be whole. Not only is that a myth, but it is a tragic form of self-robbery. It is forfeiting the day in the vain hope of some future panacea.

The journey IS the destination, and today IS my life. God and God's Magic are always only in the right now, never in the future. My friend, Leon, puts it beautifully, by stating that if he chooses to go into the future, God says, "Have a good time, Leon. I'll be here when you get back."

I pray to realize that now is both my destination and the only reality I will ever know.

I love you all.

November 25

Good morning.

Our keynote is: "Humbly say to ourselves many times today, 'Thy will be done'..."

The Thought for the Day points out that comparing ourselves to others will poison the spirit.

I have an ego disorder which lies at the heart of my alcoholism and my overall spiritual malady. Without Divine Intervention, my twisted ego demands such self-obsession that I am constantly comparing myself to others.

The only possible results of those comparisons are that I will feel either prideful or wallow in self-pity.

As an egomaniac with an inferiority complex, I can insanely experience both extremes at the same time.

Early on, I was told that the only valid comparison I can ever make is to compare myself today with myself the last day I drank.

That perspective replaces destructive comparison with liberating gratitude.

If I take the action necessary to invite Divine Intervention, I am able to maintain that angle of approach and live in much less danger of pride and/or self-pity.

I find The Magic in maintaining a grateful angle of approach and refraining from comparisons.

I love you all.

November 26

Good morning.

Our keynote is: "Pray to seek to love, comfort, and understand..."

The Thought for the Day discusses freedom from our character defects.

After a few years of immersion in the AA fellowship and seeking to do and live the steps, my mind and ego still often urged me to do the wrong thing.

I was quite discouraged until I realized that I had made great progress by not acting on the thoughts, feelings, and beliefs I had considered character defects.

An even more important realization followed. I came to see that my thoughts, feelings, and beliefs hurt no one and leave no footprint on reality. I no longer consider them character defects.

My character defects are now my behavior, not what drifts through my mind.

Further, I am convinced that the most spiritual thing I can do is behave properly when I want to do the exact opposite. I can control my actions, but not my mind.

There is freedom and magic in judging myself by the standard God and my fellows judge me, which is by my behavior, not the old crazy picture show in my head.

I love you all.

November 27

Good morning.

Our keynote is: "Help God's kids do what they need to have done..."

The Meditation and Prayer for the Day encourage us to seek divine guidance in order to find God's will for us.

Originally, I envisioned the search for that guidance as a complex, intellect-driven process of seeking to ascertain and comprehend God's overall plan for my life.

I have found the reality to be far more simple and to require more childlike faith, trust, and obedience than intellectual understanding.

The only glimpse of God's will I ever really get is in the absolute right now for my own next action. Frequently, things happen which completely change what I expect God's will to be in the next five seconds. Yet, I waste time guessing at God's will for next Tuesday or ten years from now.

My only conduit to the will of The Creator is the Spark of the Divine which resides in each of us. It will only show me the next stitch; it will never reveal the pattern in advance.

I find The Magic in coming as a trusting little child and heeding my Divine Parent's guidance for each single stitch, even though I can't see what lies beyond.

I love you all.

November 28

Good morning.

Our keynote is "Persistence".

The theme of today's Meditation and Prayer is gratitude.

When I was newly sober, everyone seemed to be telling me that I needed to be grateful. Because my default position is to view the way I feel as the most important thing in the world, I thought they were telling me I needed to FEEL grateful all the time.

As I began to realize that my thoughts, feelings, and beliefs are not nearly as important as my actions, I developed an entirely new understanding of what it means to be grateful. It means to BEHAVE gratefully. Today, I am as grateful as I act... no more, no less.

The feeling of gratitude is pleasant and makes it easier to behave gratefully, but otherwise, it has no impact on reality.

Actions consistent with gratitude have a great positive impact on reality and will ultimately reward me with the warm, peaceful feeling of gratitude. Under my old conception of gratitude, I had no control over whether I was grateful, but by my current standard, magically, it is completely within my control.

I love you all.

November 29

Good morning.

Our keynote is "Courtesy".

Today's Prayer asks that we may live close to both God and others.

It has proved impossible for me to be close to God while abusing, resenting, hating, or ignoring my fellow men and women. I cannot be discourteous or dishonest and spiritual at the same time.

Conversely, I have come to believe that human relationships are ultimately impossible for me if I am totally estranged from or in disharmony with God and the Divine Spark. God's other children are the only tangible interaction I have with The Divine. What I do for or to my fellows, I do for or to my God.

My relationship with God and my relationships with others are magically linked. If I am not right with my fellows, I cannot be right with God. If I am not right with God, I cannot be right with my fellows.

I love you all.

November 30

Good morning.

Our keynote is "Gratitude".

The Prayer for the Day asks that our spirits may be in harmony with God's Spirit.

Prayer is the necessary threshold to Divine Harmony, but my spirit doesn't soar into harmony with God's just because I pray for it.

If my prayers are to produce results, I usually must follow them by persistently seeking to take each single stitch as the Divine Spark directs.

As with most things, God requires my cooperation.

It opened my eyes when I was asked years ago, "How do you turn a toothache over to God?". Before I could think of an answer, the person said, "You go to a dentist!".

The Divine Spark (that part of God which is in each one of us) tells me the next right action. If I ignore or willfully act contrary to its guidance, I cannot maintain a meaningful relationship with God. Harmony, peace, and serenity will elude me.

The Magic is in the partnership of God's power and grace with my persistent, faithful action.

I love you all.

DECEMBER

December 1

Good morning.

Our keynote is "Courtesy".

Today's Meditation and Prayer urge us to be compassionate and sympathetic.

Before sobriety, I judged myself by my feelings and believed frequent feelings of pity somehow made me a good and caring person. Today, I know such a belief to be self-centered nonsense.

Acting to help others is where compassion, sympathy and the spiritual value lie.

Ironically, the value is even greater if I proffer the help despite selfishly not wanting to do so. However, the act is largely spoiled if I communicate, explicitly or implicitly, my reluctance.

Conversely, if I tear up with emotion and my heart aches for another's plight, but fail to do what I reasonably can to ease their suffering, I am devoid of compassion.

If I take the proper action, despite my selfish desires, magically, God will lead me to feel the compassion reflected by my behavior. I will have, once again, behaved my way into right thinking and feeling by adding my action to God's grace and power.

I love you all.

December 2

Good morning.

Our keynote is "Gratitude".

Today's Prayer asks that we may strive to fulfill God's vision for us.

Believing I had figured out God's long-term vision for me was ego-driven folly and led only to futility and chaos.

I am convinced that God's will and vision for me is simply to take one stitch at a time as guided by the Divine Spark. While doing so, I will not see the pattern being formed by the single stitches.

When seeking to stitch as directed, I believe I am, at that moment, fulfilling God's vision for me. I am just never shown the finished product in advance.

One errant stitch, promptly followed by a proper one, doesn't separate me from God's will. Errant stitches and correction are part of God's vision for me. However, a willful SECOND stitch in the same wrong direction will separate me from God and set me back on the path of self-will.

The Magic is in coming right back to the Divine Spark's guidance after each errant stitch.

Persistence is the key!

I love you all.

December 3

Good morning.

Our keynote is "Humility".

Today's Meditation begins with, "Fret not your mind with puzzles that you cannot solve."

It would be sociopathic not to feel sadness and frustration with war, birth defects, poverty, genocide, etc. The problem arises when I become lost in the unanswerable question, "Why?".

Such futile obsession turns me into a cynic and destroys my ability to help with the things that are within my power.

At least in this life, my actual knowledge of God's will and my power are limited to my own next action.

Accepting those limits of my understanding and power calms my mind and soul; it slows the drain of energy and time that flows from fretting over things I can neither understand nor control.

Magically, the humility of accepting that I can understand and do so little makes me far more effective in doing what I can to make the world a tiny bit better, one stitch at a time.

I love you all.

December 4

Good morning.

Our keynote is "Honesty".

Today's Meditation warns us not to seek the praise and notice of the world.

I have found seeking the world's adulation to be a fool's errand because it is a craving that cannot be satisfied. The quest for the world's approval and applause is a form of seeking to be loved, comforted, and understood by others, rather than seeking to love, comfort, and understand them.

I have found it to be a spiritual law that if I seek those things, I will never feel I have enough of them. Mark Twain summed it up beautifully by saying, "I have been complimented many times, and it always makes me uncomfortable. I never feel they have said enough."

The Magic is in seeking to give my entire interest, attention, and love to others, rather than seeking the same from them. Only then will I feel loved, comforted, and understood to my satisfaction. It is part of the Divine Paradox.

I love you all.

December 5

Good morning.

Our keynote is: "Humbly say to ourselves many times today, 'Thy will be done',...".

Today's Meditation and Prayer tell us to give our best to others according to their need, rather than our opinion of what they deserve. We are also urged to give of ourselves, not just advice.

When advice is explicitly or implicitly requested and lovingly and prayerfully given, it can be very helpful. But often just giving advice is ego-driven and based on intellect and psychology. It generally costs the advisor little.

If not solicited, advice is always received as criticism and often is perceived as hostility.

Giving of myself frequently involves praying to love, comfort, and understand until I am giving the other child of God my entire interest, attention, and love. Such giving of self is often inconvenient and usually includes sacrifice. However, it is also of immeasurable value to the giver. It is sharing experience and assets, not just regurgitating platitudes.

When giving only advice, I am, at best, an unqualified counselor. But magically, when giving of myself, I may briefly become a channel for God's love, bounty, and wisdom.

I love you all.

December 6

Good morning.

Our keynote is: "Pray to seek to love, comfort, and understand, ...".

Today's Meditation and Prayer declare temptation to be inevitable. We are advised to spiritually prepare for temptation's onslaught and to never caress it upon arrival.

I am tempted anytime I am attracted to doing the wrong thing instead of taking the next stitch as directed by the Divine Spark.

Each time I do the right thing, despite wanting to do the opposite, I become better armed for my next skirmish with temptation. It is spiritual bodybuilding.

Conversely, each little errant or defiant stitch makes it remarkably harder to return to harmony with the Spark.

The Magic is in realizing that temptation is but an opportunity for spiritual exercise and has only the power I give it.

Succumbing to temptation is a character defect, but being tempted is not. Fleeting temptation doesn't have to be a big deal. Its visitation and the overcoming of it by right action are the natural pattern of spiritual growth.

I love you all.

December 7

Good morning.

Our keynote is "Help God's kids do what they need to have done..."

The Thought for the Day asks if we are tolerant of other people's mistakes.

Living on high alert for flaws and shortcomings in my fellows and the world ensures that I will find them in abundance. It makes me a resentful cynic living in a harsh, dangerous, and chaotic universe.

On the other hand, maintaining God consciousness and repetitively praying to seek to love, comfort, and understand others, rather than demanding that they love, comfort, and understand me, transforms the people and the world around me. It does so by magnifying the good in people and in God's World.

I then see much less that must be tolerated and am far more able to live the AA Code, which is "Love and tolerance of others".

That angle of approach allows me to live usefully and happily as a magical creature in God's Magic World.

I love you all.

December 8

Good morning.

Our keynote is "Persistence".

Today's Prayer asks that I may find a rightful place in the world.

Before sobriety, I never felt I belonged except when assisted by alcohol or another crutch. Egomania, coupled with an inferiority complex, kept me from comfortably being a fellow among fellows.

Without Divine Intervention, I still have no peers. I will feel above people, I will feel below them, or, insanely, I will feel both at the same time.

However, bringing God into my human interactions and focusing on others changes everything. Instead of obsessing on how I am perceived, I can give my entire interest, attention, and love to another person while seeking to love, comfort, and understand them.

When doing so, I no longer feel like a solitary alien. I am a fellow among fellows, comfortably at home in God's Magic World with God's other magical creatures.

I love you all.

December 9

Good morning.

Our keynote is "Courtesy".

Today's Meditation and Prayer examine the restlessness and dissatisfaction that too often dominate our lives.

It has been said that we all have a God-shaped hole inside us that can only be filled by realizing God.

The word "realize" has been critical for me. It is a form of the word "real" and means far more than simply "to know" or "to believe in". It means that God has been brought into reality inside me.

Merely giving lip service to faith while continuing to try to manage my life will not dispel restlessness and dissatisfaction.

God becomes real only when I behave consistently with the reality and guidance of God, one stitch at a time. When I persist in faithfully stitching, restlessness and dissatisfaction are replaced with peace of mind and purpose.

Then, magically, the reality of God will perfectly fill the hole in my soul.

I love you all.

December 10

Good morning.

Our keynote is "Humility".

Today's Meditation and Prayer emphasize the importance of maintaining consciousness of God. Persistently returning to awareness of God has proved to be the closest thing to a panacea in my life. God consciousness is the foundation of any usefulness, sobriety, success, or peace I have known.

I never get myself in trouble while thinking of God. Anything I can do to remind me of God or reinforce the Divine Reality is of great value. Fleetingly holding doors for God, putting in place tangible reminders (e.g., a rubber band on my wrist), and using Emmett Fox's Golden Key are just a few of the things which help me keep God in mind.

Perhaps nothing is more effective than humbly saying to myself many times each day, "Thy will be done". Suggestions on how to maintain God consciousness have proved to be my treasure map to The Magic.

I love you all.

December 11

Good morning.

Our keynote is "Gratitude".

Today's reading suggests receiving each day as a joyous sunrise gift to be used to serve God and other people. That angle of approach, I believe, is the heart of all true spirituality...gratitude and service. My greatest self-robbery is taking the priceless gift of a day as a living, sober human being for granted.

I have squandered far too many days oblivious to God's Magic. In that spiritual ignorance, I see only drudgery and self-interest. I am blind to The Magic. However, mere awareness that human life is magic is not enough. If I selfishly try to use the gift only for my pleasure and comfort, The Magic will evaporate. But if I use the day properly, by seeking to serve God and my fellows, The Magic will remain in and all around me. I will have honored God's precious gift of the day.

My experience is that behaving as one grateful to God and seeking to serve others is the recipe for usefulness, peace, and joy.

I love you all.

December 12

Good morning.

Our keynote is "Honesty".

Today's Meditation and Prayer declare that love will drive fear from our lives. My intellect doesn't fully understand how that works, but my experience absolutely proves its validity. I can, of course, see how faith and the love of God protect us from fear.

The miracle I don't understand is how fears of financial insecurity, health problems, mortality, loss of a relationship, etc., flee when I begin taking loving action toward my fellows. Just feeling love for others doesn't necessarily protect me from fear. In fact, feeling love without action can render me especially fearful of something bad befalling the beloved or the relationship. It is action consistent with love, much more than the feeling of love, which armors me against fear.

I don't need to understand how the internet or cell phones work to depend on and use those things. The same is true of using loving action to magically expel fear. It works. It really does!

I love you all.

December 13

Good morning.

Our keynote is "Persistence".

The Thought for the Day attributes the unique success of Alcoholics Anonymous to the fact that it is based on a sincere desire to help other people. In my experience, any spiritual fellowship or program based on doing for others is more likely to flourish than those otherwise focused.

Other than the physical allergy to, and mental obsession with, alcohol, what we call "alcoholism" is, I believe, actually the universal malady of humankind. It is selfishness and self-centeredness. Therefore, it cannot be effectively treated by any form of self-obsession.

Concentrating on my relationship with God is necessary, but to bring that relationship into full reality, I must turn my attention to helping God's other children. There is little magic to be found by locking myself in a closet with God. If I am to know the full measure of spiritual bounty, I must persistently seek to help God's kids do what they need to have done. "The spiritual life is not a theory; we have to live it."

I love you all.

December 14

Good morning.

Our keynote is: "Humbly say to ourselves many times each day, 'Thy will be done,...'."

When weary of the world's stress and turmoil, today's reading urges us to retire into the quiet contemplation of God. Many times I have started the morning with serenity only to quickly lose it in the storms of the day.

Too often I have forfeited such days by doggedly continuing to swim upstream in the world's chaos. However, The Magic has frequently been restored to seemingly lost days by the simple expediency of starting the day over. I can do that anywhere and anytime.

If necessary, I can start a day over in a crowd, but, circumstances permitting, it is preferable to briefly drop down on my knees. I can do that by my desk, in a restroom, or wherever is available. I can then spend a couple of minutes in prayer and thoughts of God. After that brief respite with my Creator, my big deals recede into little ones, the disturbances in my soul and mind abate, and I am back in God's Magic with a brand new day.

I love you all.

December 15

Good morning.

Our keynote is: "Courtesy".

Today's Meditation and Prayer address the dull, gray days when joy and harmony with both God and our fellows seem to have deserted us.

Sometime ago, I related my experience with a professional poker player who said that the entire difference between success and failure lay in how he played the worst hands he was dealt.

I suspect my ultimate success or failure largely depends on how I behave during the dull, gray days. When I let go of the infantile idea that I should always feel good and instead try to bring joy to my fellows, I am ultimately rewarded with the return of joy. When I behave as guided by the Divine Spark, I begin to regain harmony with God and those around me.

My ego disorder tells me that the way I feel is the most important thing in the world. However, the value of each day is determined by what I do that day. How I felt while doing it never leaves a footprint on reality.

The Magic is in behaving on the dull, gray days just as I do when filled with joy and harmony.

I love you all.

December 16

Good morning.

Our keynote is: "Pray to seek to love, comfort, and understand..."

Today's Meditation and Prayer beautifully explain the futility of directly seeking my own happiness. I tried it for 37 years with disastrous results. My ego disorder is such that I am capable of turning even the spiritual program of recovery into merely a tool for my own sobriety, peace, and happiness. In doing so, I rob myself and miss the real purpose of the AA program and spirituality. Sobriety, peace, and happiness will be found along the 12 Step path. But, I can only receive them in full measure as a byproduct of serving my fellows and God.

The basis of my alcoholism is self-centeredness. I cannot effectively treat it by any form of self-obsession. I have an entire wardrobe for self-centeredness, which includes security, responsibility, psychological, and even spiritual clothing. My ego insists that self-obsession is proper when dressed so appealingly.

As usual, my ego deceives me. Self-obsession remains a futile attempt to put out a fire with gasoline. I never find The Magic by thinking about myself.

I love you all.

December 17

Good morning.

Our keynote is: "Help God's kids do what they need to have done..."

The Prayer for the Day asks that I may live this 24 hours with faith, hope, and love. In early sobriety, I believed that FEELING faith, hope, and love was living with them. I now know that I am not living with those things just because I feel them. My feelings, in and of themselves, have no impact on anything except me, unless I childishly allow my feelings to dictate my behavior.

Thankfully, it is also true that I can live with faith, hope, and love on the gray days when I don't feel much of those things. It is my prayer today that God will help me BEHAVE faithfully, hopefully, and lovingly, regardless of how I am feeling. Magically, I eventually feel the things which I persistently do.

Only my actions ever leave a footprint on reality, and it is by those actions alone that the world and, I believe, God judge me.

I love you all.

December 18

Good morning.

Our keynote is "Persistence".

The Prayer for the Day asks that I may not worry over the limitations of my human mind. Human cognitive abilities are nothing short of magic. And, to be a living, sober, and healthy human being for a day is a gift beyond measure. However, acceptance of the extreme limits of my understanding and power is necessary in order to be fully in harmony with God's Magic.

My understanding of God's will is limited to my own single next stitch (i.e., action). That next stitch is also, ultimately, the only thing in the universe under my control. However, my minuscule understanding and power turn out to be understanding and power enough. Acceptance of those limitations frees me from trying to comprehend the future, death, sickness, war, hunger, etc. That freedom, in turn, enables me to better address everything God puts on my plate.

My proper role is to rejoice in and, by my behavior, honor what I CAN understand and do, while leaving the rest in God's hands.

I love you all.

December 19

Good morning.

Our keynote is "Courtesy".

The Thought for the Day discusses skeptics and agnostics who say it is impossible for us to find the answer to life. I came to AA beyond skeptical and as an evangelical agnostic.

In April of 1981, a loving God, whom I had never acknowledged, gave me the life-saving gift of beginning to voluntarily follow directions even though they were contrary to my thoughts, feelings, and beliefs. As a result, the twin miracles of AA's second step occurred in my life.

First, as soon as I began behaving like one who believed, I started getting the benefits of belief. Second, through that same faithful behavior, I indeed came to believe and faith found me. Magically and ironically, I experience the answer to life by accepting the extreme limitations of my ability to comprehend it.

I cannot understand spirituality, I must first behave spiritually and then, as a result, I experience spirituality. "The spiritual life is not a theory. We have to live it."

I love you all.

December 20

Good morning.

Our keynote is "Gratitude".

Today's reading is about my archenemy, fear. My most effective defenses against it are the following:

1. Maintaining God consciousness. Fear recoils from the thought of God.
2. Staying in the moment. I am alone, without God, and have no defense against fear in the past or future.
3. Avoiding "big deals". Even good big deals can terrify me.
4. Acting promptly. Procrastination guarantees fear.
5. Seeking to love, comfort, and understand others, while giving them my entire interest, attention, and love. I am rarely afraid unless I'm thinking about myself.

Persistently using those tools, while not doing things which figuratively put rattlesnakes under my bed, keeps me consciously connected with God's Magic. Fear cannot flourish in God's Magic World of faith.

I love you all.

December 21

Good morning.

Our keynote is "Kindness".

Today's Meditation and Prayer are about what I call the Divine Spark. It is called many things, including "conscience", "moral compass", "small voice", and "The Holy Spirit". By any name, it is the little part of God which is in each of us and guides our actions only one stitch at a time.

God most surely lights my way, but it is with a penlight for the next step only: never with a searchlight illuminating 90 days down the path.

Seeking to come as a little child and heed the Divine Spark, without knowledge or understanding of the pattern God has ordained, has been the guiding principle of my life for many years.

My ego and brain don't want to accept that the key to a useful, successful, peaceful, and joyous life is that simple. They clamor that, surely, if I am to have such a life, it must primarily be the fruit of my intellect and will!

Yet, my experience is that seeking to let go of all my self-determined objectives, in favor of a child-like obedience, magically, is my path to successful living.

I love you all.

December 22

Good morning.

Our keynote is "Humility".

The Prayer for the Day asks that we not be overwhelmed by the fear of evil. It is usually venturing into the future which allows the fear of evil, and all things negative, to paralyze me.

As my friend, Leon, says, "If I go into the future, or the past, God says, 'Have a good time. I will be here when you get back'." God never gives me the strength to handle the future. I have wasted many prayers by asking God on Thursday to help me cope with Friday.

Those prayers have never borne fruit and I doubt they ever will. God always gives me the strength to handle the right now. It is when I go into the future or the past that I am alone and unprotected. God's Magic can only be found here and now!

I love you all.

December 23

Good morning.

Our keynote is "Honesty".

The Prayer for the Day asks that I may think, speak and act constructively while bringing something good into every situation.

Prayer and meditation in the morning lay the essential foundation for such a constructive day. However, my behavior throughout that day will determine whether God adds the divine power and grace necessary for constructive living. I need to be persistently courteous, try to maintain God consciousness and seek to avoid both conflict and giving unsolicited advice.

If, in addition, I try to give each person my entire interest, attention and love, while silently praying to seek to love, comfort, and understand, God's Magic comes to bear. Then, I may find myself thinking, speaking and acting constructively, while bringing something good into every situation.

I love you all.

December 24

Good morning.
Our keynote is "Gratitude".

The Meditation for the Day declares that, while gratitude and service are necessary, they are not quite enough. There must also be sacrifice. Giving my time and resources to others is pleasant when I have the extra time and resources and feel warmly toward the recipient. However, giving under those circumstances has a component of selfishness.

Doing what I want to do when it doesn't inconvenience me is of limited spiritual value. Giving of my time, resources, and love to those I don't particularly want to give when I don't feel I have enough of anything to spare is immediately painful. However, giving in those circumstances is the most spiritually valuable and ultimately rewarding giving. Magically, making the short term sacrifice eventually expands my time and resources and grows my love.

In the end, giving when it hurts brings the most joy of all. One sentence in today's Meditation has given me much comfort and increased my usefulness. It urges us to not try to actively combat evil, but rather, simply try to ignore it.

I love you all.

Christmas Day

Good morning and Merry Christmas!

Our keynote is "Pray to seek to love, comfort, and understand..."

The Thought for the Day urges recovered alcoholics to contemplate the miracle of God having brought us up out of the abyss. Alcoholism is, of course, not the only face of the abyss. It comes in countless guises and, I believe, lurks within each of us.

My ego and self-obsession are the pathway to the abyss. When they assume control and turn my attention totally inward, erasing thoughts of God and helping my fellows, the abyss is the only possible destination.

I pray today that I will remember that God lets me carry, along with the abyss, the key to liberation from it. The key is simply focusing my behavior on serving God and my fellows, rather than obsessing over myself. Persisting along the path of love and service will lead me out of the abyss into the sunlight of God's Magic World.

I love you all.

December 26

Good morning.

Our keynote is "Help God's kids do what they need to have done..."

The Meditation for the Day tells us to carry the message of recovery but to accept that we lack the power to deliver it. By accepting my limitations and leaving the results to God, I am able to do my best without urgency or strain. Failure to accept my lack of power makes a big deal of myself and hobbles me in my efforts to be helpful. Refusing to fret over those I cannot help is not a lack of caring. It is an act of humility that frees me to help those who are receptive. I must also recoil from any temptation to give myself any credit for those who do embrace the message and go on to become models of recovery. If I have quietly, persistently, and lovingly carried the message, I have done my work regardless of the outcome. God and the other person are in charge of whether The Magic happens and the message I have carried is delivered.

I love you all.

December 27

Good morning.

Our keynote is "Kindness".

Today's reading addresses the development of new and better lives as we persist along AA's spiritual path. My first nine years of sobriety, I believed it necessary to visualize the new me and, with God's help, work to bring my vision into reality. My life improved, but I began to realize that I can't comprehend who and what God would have me become.

God won't show me where I should go, but will show me, one little step at a time, how to get there. So, I began to persistently concentrate on only the next stitch as guided by the Divine Spark. This brought even more progress.

Finally, in the last few years, I am realizing that coming as a little child, concentrating on the next stitch, and leaving the results to God is not just the path to a better life. It is the better life. The journey itself is The Magic and the destination. As long as I persist along the path, I am already home!

I love you all.

December 28

Good morning.

Our keynote is "Persistence".

The Prayer for the Day asks that I may feel close enough to God to depend on Divine help. As with most of my prayers, I must follow that one with action if I am to reap the full benefit of God's grace and power. When hungry, if I lock myself in a closet and pray for food, it is not likely that a hotdog will squirt through the keyhole.

I need to put myself in the vicinity of food after praying. Regarding today's prayer, I cannot feel divinely protected unless I first maintain consciousness of God. I can prompt that consciousness by leaving myself notes, holding doors for God, using Emmett Fox's Golden Key, or simply putting a rubber band around my wrist.

Anything which reminds me to think of God is helpful. The Magic often flows from the partnership of God's power and grace with my prayer and action.

I love you all.

December 29

Good morning.

Our keynote is "Courtesy".

Today's reading emphasizes an aspect of our partnership with God which has transformed both me and the world I live in. It tells us that all our work with people should be based in prayer, and that saying a little prayer before speaking or trying to help will make us more effective.

My most frequent and effective prayer before and during human contact is to seek to love, comfort, and understand and, often more importantly, not to seek love, comfort, and understanding for myself. Merely praying to be, and then actually being, courteous fosters harmony and love. Praying, "Thy will be done", or to speak the quiet, loving truth has expelled "big dealism" and stress from many encounters.

The Magic is in consciously bringing God into my human contacts, not in the particular words I pray.

I love you all.

December 30

Good morning.

Our keynote is "Gratitude".

Today's Meditation and Prayer warn against trying to live for ourselves alone. I tried it for 37 years and, unless I persist in the action necessary to maintain my spiritual condition, I will fall back into it today.

My ego finds serving myself terribly attractive. However, it didn't work then and it doesn't work now. Trying to fill the emptiness inside me with money, things, power, and the world's applause is truly a fool's errand. I have a God-shaped hole in me that can be filled by nothing except God.

When I try to stitch as directed by the Divine Spark and be useful to my fellows, the Divine Paradox does its magic; the more I forget myself and think of God and others, the better I am served. By focusing on giving rather than acquiring for myself, I receive more than I could have imagined.

I love you all.

December 31

Happy New Year's Eve!

Our keynote is "Humility".

The Meditation for the Day suggests reviewing this past year. In doing so, I clearly see that my thoughts, feelings, and beliefs are nowhere in the record book of 2022.

Only the consequences of my behavior throughout the year now have any reality. I can also see that my greatest progress came when I properly handled the "bad hands" (i.e., the situations which seemed so terrible that I didn't even want to think about them). It is apparent, in retrospect, that God has woven many of the lowest points of this extraordinary year into a beautiful tapestry.

God's Magic is most clearly seen where I took the next stitch as the Divine Spark guided, despite my doubt, fear, and pride. Doing the right thing when I don't want to do it and/or am afraid brings God's power and grace to bear on reality. Then, my past reluctance, fear and ego wounds (which felt so real and important) amount to nothing.

I love you all.